Dancing At
My Funeral

Dancing At My Funeral

Maxie Dunnam

ILLUSTRATIONS BY JERRY DUNNAM

FOREWORD BY BRUCE LARSON

The Upper Room

A special Upper Room edition published by arrangement with FORUM HOUSE Publishers/Atlanta

DANCING AT MY FUNERAL . . .

A special edition for The Upper Room published by arrangement with FORUM HOUSE Publishers/Atlanta containing the complete text of the original hardcover edition.

Forum House edition published June 1973
Special Edition for The Upper Room published September 1973

Printed in the United States of America
Library of Congress catalog card number 72-86155

A listing of reference sources for which we give grateful acknowledgment can be found at the end of this book.

UR-297-10-10-0174

First Printing—June 1973
Second Printing—October 1973
Third Printing—January 1974

Dedication

To our parents,
Murdock and Cora Dunnam,
Gerald and Lora Morris,
with deep joy and thanksgiving
for your constant love.

And with appreciation to the
community of West Anaheim United Methodist Church,
and especially to those who have contributed in a
specific way to this book: Jim Boltz, Marj Boltz,
Sue Collins, Ron Crandall, Dick Miller, Nan Moore,
Dawn Smith, and Laurie Stewart.

CONTENTS

FOREWORD by Bruce Larson

This is an exciting time in which to be alive. Change is the thing in every area of life, but nowhere more evident than in the new way Christians are coming to view life as it was meant to be under the Lordship of Christ.

Maxie Dunnam is one of the architects of the new thing God is doing in this time. A pastor, a leader and a pioneer, he is helping many discover a fresh experience of God's grace and man's potential.

One of the marks of this new day is the discovery of a new kind of theology. The old theology was marked by a totally objective view of God and man, while the theology of the era we are entering now is marked by a more subjective and clinical view of sin and grace and wholeness. Both of these dimensions of Christian truth are important, but in the past we have been much too aware of only the objective.

Historically, the subjective has always been a basic and a recurring theme. Leaders in the Church have been concerned about the shape of life inside and the journey inward. The degree and depth and integrity of the journey inward shape our journey outward and our degree of healthy participation in the journey outward.

This book by my friend Maxie Dunnam is about Maxie's own past. It's a book of autobiography, personal history and deep feelings. It takes into account the fact that all of us are a very real product of those early shaping forces in our lives. Maxie is now free by the grace of God to look back and to look within and to literally dance at the funeral of the past that has haunted him. He now finds in his past the fruitful seeds of his new life and his new ministry. The past for all of us is not something to be hidden, but something to be celebrated. The author reminds us that our Lord said that the Kingdom of God is within. It is within us that we begin to find the truest understanding of the shape of grace and of the new creation.

Maxie Dunnan has written a book that is in the tradition of St. Paul, St. Augustine, John Woolman and Keith Miller. It is a guidepost and an encouragement to Christians moving into this new age. It is my hope that many participants in God's great adventure today will read this book and be encouraged to look within and to dance.

Bruce Larson

PREFACE...

A
DANCING
TRIP

The plane from San Francisco to Los Angeles was crowded. From the seats that were left, I chose one beside a teenage girl who seemed to be cowering in a corner. She had a book in her lap, and as I settled down, I caught the title, *How To Make It in the Woods.*

I knew that many young people were dropping out and seeking a simple life removed from the·city, but I didn't know that the migration warranted a how-to book on the subject. Intrigued, I engaged the young lady in conversation.

In talking to her I once again reaffirmed my belief that the Spirit will work in relationships whenever we are open—open to ourselves and open to the other person. This young woman and I had a beautiful hour of sharing, a precious period that had an eternal dimension because real communication—*soul* communication—took place.

When she sensed my genuine interest, 17-year-old Sally talked earnestly and freely about her "trip"—her effort to find meaning in life. Then, about 20 minutes before we landed, she asked me, "And what is *your* trip?" I didn't answer immediately. Then I said, "I'm on a *dancing* trip." Her eyes brightened. She wanted to know more, and I shared more. In fact, I shared the essence of what I want to share with you in this book.

Yes, I'm on a *dancing* trip! That's odd, really, for I have no technical knowledge of dancing nor is "the dance" part of my culture. For me, dancing is a symbol, and I hope that as you read, you'll come to understand this symbol and why it's so important to me. I *feel* it! Deep down, I feel it!

But about the title. Am I dancing at my *funeral?* Yes! Funerals I know about. I've always known about them. In rural Mississippi, we weren't protected from whatever damage they're supposed to inflict upon children. Funerals were part of our culture, like going to town on Saturday, Fourth-Sunday sings, summer revival meetings, cakewalks at school socials, and smoking rabbit tobacco behind the barn. Also, as a minister, I've conducted hundreds of funerals.

Funerals are about death. Death has many faces. One face is *spiritual* death, the things within us that must die if we are to live. Features of this face include resentment, guilt, self-hate, and remorse. These things will cripple us, make us less than men and women—and prematurely bury us if we do not bury them. And then there is *physical* death, over which we may have little control and ultimately have *no* control. An accident stamps out a life, or a life passes in a natural way. Someone we love is with us no more. And our own death—we can't understand that until it happens.

Funerals are about death; *dancing* is about life. My trip is *dancing at my funeral.* Dancing when I have the courage to resist forces that would bury me and am somehow given the power to bury them, instead. Dancing when I bury some part of me that doesn't deserve to live—some ritual that is no longer meaningful, some security blanket that no longer supports, some phony approach to life, some superficial relationship, some crutch, or game, or mask.

I am dancing in the face of tragedy over which I have no control except to trust God and life and circumstance. I am able to live in the presence of death because I trust myself as a victor rather than victim.

The dance and the funeral are *symbols* for my trip. But symbols may be very real!

I invite you to join me on my trip. Dance with me!

Maxie Dunnam
Anaheim, California
1973

Chapter 1

Old Pappy Time Is A Picking My Pocket

The ridiculous and the sublime of our experience often are bound together by a cord of memory—you recall the one and the other comes sliding out of its storage rack and replays, too.

Whenever I read the 90th Psalm, which I often do at funerals, the congregation must think it strange when a half-smile plays across my face. This expression is inappropriate and unintended. What happens is that this sublime psalm invariably triggers a replaying of a ridiculous song which I heard on a cold winter's night many years ago.

It may have been during the Christmas holidays—at any rate, I was driving from Mississippi to Georgia. I became exhausted, and fearing that I might doze off, I stopped at a roadside cafe to energize myself with coffee.

I'm not talking about a Howard Johnson-type of restaurant, but a truck stop. You know the type, standing there alongside a desolate stretch of road, slumbering by day but coming alive at night to beckon you with its winking neon eyes.

Maybe it's just me, but loneliness seems to pervade such places and the people who frequent them. There's always a juke box, and it's packed with loneliness, too. Its songs tell of hurt and heartbreak, unrequited love and lost hopes. I'm not knocking these songs, understand. Some deal with life rather authentically. For example, when Bobbie Gentry sings "Ode to Billie Joe," you share the hurt, frustration, and guilt of the bereft young lover even though you've likely never been near the fateful Tallahatchie River Bridge. Each of us has his or her own Tallahatchie Bridge.

Although it's been fully 15 years since I stopped in at that roadside cafe, the song that I heard there keeps coming back to mind. I had never heard it before and I've never heard it since. I don't remember the words, but I remember the tune, the twanging, nasal voice of the singer, and the oft-repeated title line: "Old Pappy Time Is A'Picking My Pocket."

This song wasn't a classical art form; nevertheless, there's an immortal thought in that title, "Old Pappy Time Is A'Picking My Pocket," and it has been a burr under the saddle of my memory all these years.

But back to the sublime, the 90th Psalm. Do you remember how it goes?

(Verses 1, 2, 4, 5, 6, 9, 12 RSV.)

Lord, thou hast been our dwelling place
    in all generations.
Before the mountains were brought forth, or
    ever thou hadst formed the earth and the
    world, from everlasting to everlasting
thou art God.
. . . . .
For a thousand years in thy sight
    are but as yesterday when it is past,
. . . . .
like grass which is renewed in the morning:
in the morning it flourishes and is renewed;
    in the evening it fades and withers.
. . . .
Our years come to an end like a sigh.
. . . .
So teach us to number our days
    that we may get a heart of wisdom.

"Old Pappy Time Is A'Picking My Pocket" is a ridiculous song. Who remembers it? The 90th Psalm is sublime literature which has endured through the ages. It's strange that I would associate these two, isn't it? Yet, I believe it's like this in our experience. If we will tear off the pretentious, protective wrapping and get to the core of our life-package, we will find there a strange mixture of beauty and ugliness, ecstasy and agony.

But we are not helplessly stuffed with these things. Indeed, I am walking evidence that the hell that is inside us can be turned into heaven. This is why I'm writing this book.

My change came about in the most unsuspected and even implausible way. I was going to my funeral but instead experienced my resurrection. You see, Old Pappy Time had picked my pocket for a long, long time. I don't mean that he was shoving me into fearsome old age—what he was doing was sucking out my life-juices. The unresolved conflicts of my past sapped my vitality so that I was unable to live vibrantly in the present or to contemplate the future without anxiety.

I knew with my *mind* that we can only live in the present, but that was not my *experience*. Indeed, I was stuck in my past as though my feet were planted in concrete.

There are immature and destructive ways in which people can deal with their past. One is to glory in the past as if it were some golden age which, alas, will never return. With such an attitude, we linger in the fantasies of yesterday and refuse to move up into the realities of today. And if living in the present is difficult, relating to the future is an impossibility.

My problem was just the opposite. I didn't love the past, I *hated* it. I'm not talking about hating isolated parts of my past; I hated the whole bundle. I wanted to bury my past, but I didn't respect it sufficiently to give it a decent funeral.

Some people describe themselves as "children of the Depression," meaning they were shaped by that economic era which began with the suicide-generating crash of 1929 and continued well into the New Deal. In 1934, when I was born, economic ruin still marred the face of Perry County, Mississippi.

But I suffered my depression later and in another place. My depression came over me when I moved beyond the confines of Perry County. Travel, college, and seminary provided me with windows through which I looked out upon a bright, rich world. But when I looked out the rearward windows and into my past, I saw a dull, deprived world. I felt that as a kid I had been cheated. I became resentful and bitter. Thoughts of my past put a rancid taste in my mouth.

I remember the one suit, one white shirt, and one tie with which I went to college. The suit was the least expensive that we could find in Richton. (These were not depression days, but 1951.) The occasion for its purchase was the high school senior class play. I was cast as the father of two teenagers and I had to wear a suit appropriate for my stage age.

Maybe you can imagine how I felt the first week of college when I arrived at a fraternity rush party in my drab, middle-aged attire. Amid snappily dressed college dons, I stood out like a sore thumb.

That experience was one among many that caused my resentment and bitterness to grow.

I had already begun my proving game. Despite feelings of miserable out-of-placeness, I stuck with the fraternity bit until after I had been initiated. Then I dropped. The feelings of not belonging were too great. I had proved something, however. I had proved that I *could* be a fraternity man. That pattern of empty proving was to continue for many years.

Francis Thompson experienced a "Hound of Heaven," the incessant

love of God following him. I'm sure that was my experience, too.
But another "hound" was far more real to me most of the time—a
"hound of hell." This hound, my past, dogged my heels. Its barking
threatened to reveal who I really was—a limited, underdeveloped,
uncultured, unsophisticated exile from rural Mississippi. Internally,
I began minimizing the progress that I had made; I came to feel
that the only difference between then and now was that now I was
wearing shoes.

Cold words on a cold page cannot recreate the desperation which
I suffered. Thoughts of my personal history put a rancid taste in
my mouth. And although your past is no doubt different from mine,
perhaps there is in your history some unresolved conflict that sends
shudders up and down your spine. If so, it will help you to understand
what I'm saying.

Here is how Henri Percikow in "Childhood" expressed the feelings
I'm trying to share:

Can I forget—
The barren chalked garret
In which we huddled,
Curling from cold,
Fighting for the shifting coats?
Can I forget—
The stinking cellar
where the sunshine was alien
And the orange crate bare?

Can I forget—
Mother, nursing the lame
washing the ghetto dead—
For scanty crumbs?
I can't forget
When still trapped
On the hook of greed
Warding off the hurt
Of the desperate claws.

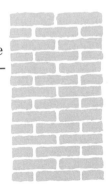

Mine was a different sort of ghetto, although it had claws which raked across my soul.

In my preadolescent days, we lived in a three-room "shotgun" house. There was a kitchen, a living room with a bed in it, and another room with two beds. I was the youngest of five children, and often I slept with the two just older than me. The heater in the living room ravenously devoured the wood that I brought in but gave out pitifully little warmth in exchange. My ghetto had grassless yards, dilapidated cars, sagging porches, and barns whose pungent odors penetrated the kitchen when the wind was blowing wrong. The toilet was inconveniently reached by a path. The "joys" of my ghetto included "commodity" butter and hand-me-down overalls. Dried lima beans were our staple food four or five times a week. A food celebration was Sunday dinner with a chicken killed from our yard. We were late getting government electricity; I read by kerosene lamp until I was in the fifth grade.

Although my life-poverty originated chiefly out of economics and geography, poverty doesn't depend upon either of these elements. For example, perhaps you yourself have endured interminable stretches of empty time, and the memory of this nothingness haunts you nowadays as a wasteland can continue to mock a parched traveler

The primary meaning of time is that there are persons who become bridges over the past and the future that you may walk in the present with meaning.

long after his rescue. Most cases of life-poverty seem to have sprung out of broken relationships. Perhaps your relationships with one or more of your parents or siblings have left you upset or unfulfilled. Are you carrying around inside you the jagged pieces of a shattered love affair or a smashed career? Do you suffer guilt because you hurt someone? Has the door to reconciliation or recovery seemingly been slammed shut by someone's death or financial collapse?

Although the terrible event itself is back there in the past, the disappointment, hurt, bitterness, or remorse which you feel is in the present. It is excruciatingly real, isn't it?

To banish the past, we can employ *repression*. I doubt that anyone has tried to repress the past (push it back even beyond consciousness) any more than I have. But repression doesn't work. There's a sinister power within the past which enables it to come twisting and contorting out of the depths of our being and into our thoughts no matter how hard we try to forget.

We can also try to overcome the past by running (and how I have run!). Some people run in disreputable ways—they take drugs, engage in illicit sex, or abandon their family. Some run in socially acceptable ways—they scramble up the ladder of success and establish a home

in the suburbs, gathering for themselves and their children a portfolio of credentials via education and memberships. They run after "the good things of life" which they couldn't afford in the past and which many *other* people can't afford in the present.

My past was pursuing me like a hound of hell, and I ran! In countless past encounters, this hound had slashed and torn me. He was always out there somewhere, sniffing me out. I lived in dread of his next attack.

Finally, it became apparent to me that I would either move to slay this beast or he would devour me. But from the temporary successes that I had experienced over the years, I recognized that I couldn't expect to rescue myself in one fell swoop; instead, I would have to begin a long and painful process—I would have to grasp this specter, handle it, examine it, even live with it. I had to convince myself that of itself the past wasn't terrifying—I was letting the past unnerve me as a child is terrorized by shadows on a bedroom wall.

The first serious step in my process of inner-self communication I took quite deliberately. I blocked out two days on my calendar and obtained use of a cabin way back in the mountains.

Being a "modern" man, I had always assumed that without noise and activity, nothing was happening. This was one of the reasons why I'd never been alone with myself for long—it seemed unproductive. Another reason was that I was afraid to be alone with myself. And although I recommend the process highly, let me caution you that until you have tried being alone and apart for two days, you have no conception of the stillness, emptiness, and penetrating loneliness.

Although my purpose was clear, I attempted to shield myself that first morning by engaging in "busy" activities. I cleaned the cabin and filled potholes in the road. Slowly, I became able to throw off my everyday compulsions and inhibitions. I ran through tall grass, waded in a cold stream, skipped rocks across a crystal pool nestled under a powerful waterfall. I wafted leaves off a cliff and watched them float to a new resting place.

I was a tow-headed boy again—barefoot, shirtless. Memories of hours spent alone on a creek bank waiting for a fish to take my bait flooded in. Being alone *then* hadn't been painful, I reflected. Why *now?*

I was becoming more at peace with myself, and finally I found courage to throw myself into my task.

It was then that those two days really became *mine.* I remembered, reflected, prayed. I cried, screamed, kicked rocks, pounded on my pillow. At other times, I recited poetry aloud or sang. All the while I was recollecting, sorting out, throwing away, keeping.

It happened the second night. It was cold and I hugged the fireplace. It was also near Christmas. Perhaps it was these connections that conjured up this relic of my past, the roadside cafe. It appeared as I saw myself driving down a desolate road. I went inside. The customers and waitresses stood or sat lifeless, like wax figures in a museum. I looked into their empty faces. Meanwhile, I was pained by the unbearable silence of the place.

There was the click of a coin and the whirring of machinery, and out of the jukebox came that loud, twanging voice singing "Old Pappy Time Is A'Picking My Pocket."

In a twinkling, the scene was gone—the curtain of my memory-theater came down. Once again I was in the cabin, alone and chilled. But there had been in that tableau a message for me, and the message remained with me.

For the first time, I saw that my past had power to undo me because I myself was energizing it. My past was *back there,* frozen in time as were these figures in the roadside cafe. The past couldn't hurt me unless I *let* it hurt me.

That night I was able to call to my mind's stage many events of the past which I had never before permitted myself to view objectively. Some memories caused me to wince, but seeing them in perspective permitted me to deal with them without either wallowing in remorse or withdrawing in pain.

I had achieved what I had come to the mountains to accomplish: to deal with my history and to purge my mind and cleanse my soul. I had stopped in my tracks and I had turned and faced that hound of hell. To my delight, I discovered that he had stopped, too. He didn't go away, but he didn't unnerve me any longer.

I became able to accept and appreciate my past. There were parts of it, I discovered, which I wanted to keep alive; there were other parts which I wanted to bury. And in this "funeral" process, I began to experience life with a freshness and a sense of purpose that had eluded me.

I was dancing at my funeral.

I came down from the mountain to my family, to begin a new life with them.

One evening not long after my mountaintop experience, I went shopping alone. In the midst of the hustle and bustle of a toy department, I felt the cold nose and hot breath of that hound of hell once again. I recalled scraggly Christmas trees, near-empty stockings, and turkey-less tables. However, I was able to call up the resources that I had gained in the mountains. Through the same process of examination, acceptance, sifting out, and putting into perspective, I was able to cope with the feelings of loneliness and resentment of this later encounter. Not only was I able to free myself, but even to rise to a higher level of self-appreciation and confidence.

On my way home, I reflected upon what had happened. Upon arriving home, I set down these lines:

> I was a child again
> > but not really a child
>
> I was a man-child
> > reduced to fantasy
> > and speechless awe
> > by what I saw
>
> The "Indy 500"
> > was a far cry
> > from the homemade truck
> > a board for a body
> > a tin can for a cab
>
> Magnet chess and checker pieces
> > that hold to shiny boards
> > were far out front
> > of games played with buttons
> > on squares penciled
> > on a cardboard box
>
> Even the "tic-tac-toe"
> > was·in fine garb
> > x's and o's in tuxedos

standing at attention
in squares neatly
scored on wooden plaques
instead of x's and o's
in common dress
standing at ease
in irregular spaces
laid out by a stubby pencil

There was Monopoly and Aggravation
and Red Baron and hundreds of
other games of chance and skill

There were Hot Wheels and Korny Kars
and Tonkas and Matchboxes
It was another world
and I was a child again

None of these fantastic toys
had ever been mine
But I remembered a little track
about two feet in diameter
and a little windup train
creeping around
(It must have been zooming then)

It provided thrills aplenty
until the spring
too tired
and too tightly wound
gave up and died

I found it in a dresser drawer
(We didn't have a tree that year)
on Christmas morning
and I knew that Santa came to
poor boys' homes, too.

I was a child again
   but not really a child
I was a man-child
   reduced to fantasy and awe
   by what I saw

I thanked God for memory
and parents who tried hard
and gave all!

That, to me, is life! To be able to look at the past with openness. To be able to deal with gashing wounds as well as gracious gifts. To be able to accept the intimate moments and the utter abandonment. Through my process of self-communication, I had become able to deal with the whole mix of my past.

Now I could acknowledge past events, appreciate them, and appropriate them for present use. I recognized that it was I who had made many decisions which in the past I had chosen to blame on others. My parents hadn't failed me; I made a "bummer" out of my past by resentment. More importantly, I was able to celebrate the fact that here and now I am a *decision-maker!*

The smell of death was giving way to the aroma of life. With Sam Keene in "To A Dancing God," I could say: "Judgment, forgiveness, and gratitude will form the alchemy which transforms the past from fate into fortune and which changes me from being a victim of causes over which I had no control to being a participant in a past which I continually reform."

My conversion and discovery of a new life-style are so precious to me that I want to share them with you. But for the moment, you may find it more profitable to lay this book aside and begin dealing with your own past.

Call up out of your past the things that hound you. Acknowledge them—write them down or discuss them with someone. Be honest. Be specific. Make a thorough self-examination. Once you have done this, pick up this book again and review your situation, using the following questions as guidelines:

What pain do you feel?

What joy?

What confusion?

What certainty?

How painful was the memory?

How crippling?

How important or superficial?

What about it do you want to keep?

What would you like to bury?

Who are the important persons?

Whom are you holding responsible?

Do you need to confess?

To forgive?

Is there anything you can do?

Is there anything you want to do?

If so, why don't you do it?

Don't repress—acknowledge! Don't run—affirm!

But a word of caution: Don't expect all your problems to vanish in a flash. Remember, self-communication and inner renewal is a *process,* an ongoing enterprise!

When the Psalmist prayed, "So teach us to number our days that we may get a heart of wisdom," he undoubtedly was talking about *all* our days—past, present, future. God is Lord of not only the present and future but also the *past.* Your present will never be the exciting, living-fully-here-and-now experience that you deserve until you confront and grapple with whatever hound of hell has been plaguing you out of the past. And God will help you do it!

If you've been feeling as though you were going to a funeral, remember: You can experience a resurrection!

The Joys of Knowing and Being Known

The impersonal appearance of a new apartment building in Munich outraged artist-photographer Peter Nemetschek and he decided to give the building a face—indeed, a community of faces. He photographed the tenants and placed life-sized portraits of them in their windows. A few tenants, huddling in their anonymity, refused to be pictured, but the vast majority cooperated. The result of this "opening of shutters" was dramatic. Tenants began talking to each other and visiting one another. Suddenly, their neighbors had become flesh and blood instead of numbers.

A picture of the "humanized" apartment building appeared in *Life*. It challenged me! It was a vivid reminder of another dimension of death and resurrection with which I had been grappling. Already, I had begun coping with that hound of hell, my depressing past, but I had not yet become willing to reveal myself to others. I felt a strange kinship with the tenants who had resisted having their pictures made and posted. I coveted the courage of the other tenants, who had been able to say, "Hey, look, here's me. You might like me, and I hope you do, but here goes!"

This picture spoke to my deepest needs, as the roadside cafe and

its haunting song did. I laid aside the magazine and began reflecting
upon my own situation. The 139th Psalm as paraphrased by Leslie
F. Brandt in "Good Lord, Where Are You?" came to mind:

O God, you know me inside out, through and through.
Every thing I do,
    every thought that flits through my mind,
    every step I take,
    every plan I make,
    every word I speak,

You know, even before these things happen.
.You know my past;
You know my future.

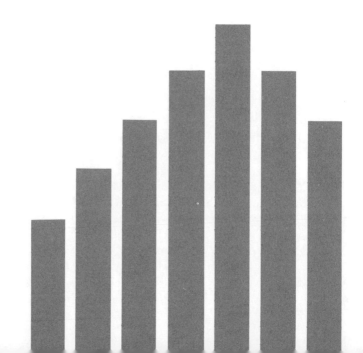

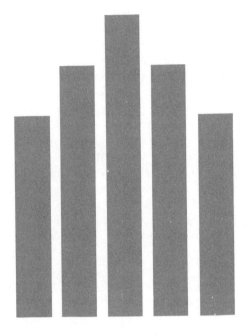

. . . .
Your knowledge of me sometimes comforts me, sometimes
    frightens me;
But always it is far beyond my comprehension.
There is no way to escape You, no place to hide.

. . . .
How frightfully and fantastically wonderful it all is!

Yes, to be known is frightfully and fantastically wonderful, I said.
I resolved then and there to be known—not just to God, but also
to the people around me. My growing ability to overcome my hang-up
over the past gave me self-confidence.

That morning, I decided to walk to the church, which is about
a mile from our home. I took along my *Life* magazine, intending
to share it with a friend. As I moved along the tree-lined sidewalk,
I began paying attention to the windows of the homes I passed. Some
residents I knew, so I could handily "paste" their portraits in their
windows. A few people were out weeding or watering their lawns,
so I could see what they looked like—I could placard their windows,
too. But I felt a sense of deep loss as I discovered that here in my
own neighborhood, there were many people I didn't know. And they
didn't know me! There were no "pictures in their windows."

There popped into my mind a formula. I'm sure the lady who
happened to come out to her mailbox at the moment thought it
strange to see me kneeling on the sidewalk. Using a knee as a desk,
I wrote the formula in a bit of white space on the back of the
magazine. When I read it over, I was so pleased that I couldn't
suppress an exclamation, "Great!"

Living depends on loving,
loving depends on knowing,
knowing depends on risking.

I've been practicing that formula ever since. Real living depends
on loving; authentic loving depends on knowing; deep knowing depends on our risking ourselves in openness.

This, then, has been another dimension of my resurrection. Step
One was to break out of the captivity of the past. Step Two was
to break out of the captivity of isolation.

We were not intended to live in isolation. We are persons only
in the context of relationships. The *will to relate* is one of our most
fundamental and powerful drives.

Howard and Charlotte Clinebell summed it up in "The Intimate
Marriage." Of the will to relate, they said: "It is more fundamental
than the striving which Sigmund Freud called the 'will to pleasure';
or that Alfred Adler described as the 'will to power', or what Victor
Frankl terms the 'will to meaning'. These strivings or desires can
be met only in relationships. Pleasure, power and meaning come into
full realization for human beings only in interpersonal relationships."

To be known, then, is essential if one is to love and live. But the
risks of being known are frightening. So very frightening! Some of
the occupants of the Munich apartment knew this fear and chose

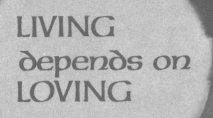

LIVING
depends on
LOVING

LOVING
depends on
KNOWING

KNOWING
depends on
RISKING

to remain anonymous. The psalmist knew this fear. So did the writer of the Book of Hebrews, in the New Testament. "It's a frightening thing," he said, "to fall into the hands of a righteous God."

And I knew this fear! I hid myself from others, and even from God. I didn't want them to know my past or my present, or my hopes and fears concerning the future.

Intellectually, we know that God is omniscient—He knows everything. That's Biblical. That's doctrinal. But emotionally we pretend that God has limited vision.

A preacher down in Mississippi had been wanting to confront a certain farmer and challenge him for God. One day, he caught the farmer out in a field and began exhorting him.

"God is omniscient," he said.

"What does that mean?"

"It means He knows everything."

The farmer seemed unimpressed. He brought out of an overalls pocket a plug of Brown Mule chewing tobacco. He began picking lint off the plug and was about to take a chew. The preacher, seizing upon this activity as a ready example, said, "Aha, God even knows you're about to take a chew of that tobacco!"

The farmer stopped short. Slowly and deliberately, he thrust the tobacco back into a pocket.

"Well," he said, a smug look spreading over his face, "I'll just fool the old man, then."

The moral of this seemingly irreverent joke is that the preacher was ineffective because he started out talking to the farmer at the lofty level of doctrine and speculation when he should have been speaking to him at the point of his experience.

The Bible is a down-to-earth book written out of human experience. It is an account of the experience of people who came to know God and were known by God; who came to know their fellow-men and to be known by their fellow-men. It's a story about people who learned how to live a life of relationships and then shared their experience with others. The psalmist, for example, reached into the depths of his soul, pulled out his most intimate feelings, and laid them out for us to know and share. He spoke out of the gut-level of his experience. The fact that God knew him made him quiver!

"Lord, Thou has searched me and known me," he said.

That's a frightening thought, that we are known by God. It's unnerving to sense that God knows:

those desires we've never permitted to surface,

those deep feelings that we keep bottled with an air-tight cap,

those secluded rooms of our being that we don't even enter, much less allow any other person to enter,

our subconscious rugs under which we sweep all sorts of dirt and dust,

the ideas that leap up and wave red flags, clamoring for expression, which we squelch,

the drives which, like jack-in-the-boxes, are constantly popping out, and are always shoved back down and the lid secured.

There are risks involved in being known by fellow humans, too. So we play hide-and-go-seek in our relationships, stretching our imaginations for fresh ways to remain hidden.

Two men were discussing income tax refunds.

"With my refund, my wife and I plan a nice vacation. What about yours?"

"I'd like that, too, but my wife isn't speaking to me. She saw my tax form and discovered that I had charged off her beauty parlor visits as a loss!"

It's painful to be found out! In his book, *Why Am I Afraid To Tell You Who I Am?*, John Powell confesses to a friend, "I'm afraid to tell you who I am, because, if I tell you who I am, you may not like who I am, and it's all that I have."

If we tell people who we are, they may not accept us; so, being known can be ruinous. But we're in a double bind here. It's equally devastating *not* to be known. Deep within us, behind all our pretenses, there's this burning desire to be known.

A young man made an appointment with me. Two years earlier, he had committed his life to Christ after a prolonged struggle. Now I wondered what was bringing him to my office again.

He came in and sat uncomfortably on the edge of his chair as if ready to depart before we got started. We exchanged pleasantries for an interminably long time. I kept trying to cut through this superficial talk, but he resisted. Finally, he spoke vaguely about his being concerned about his "life." I invited him to come right out with it.

"I must share this thing with you," he said. "But I can't!"

Perhaps his confessing that he was afraid gave him courage. He told me he was teaching a class of teenagers, and the current topic was the Christian perspective on sexuality. He had decided that he should resign because previous to his marriage (a most happy marriage), there had been an intimate relationship with a college coed. With this past, how could he counsel with youngsters about a Christian perspective on sex?

As we explored our feelings about sexuality, including his guilt and remorse, I blurted out: "Who is better qualified to talk with these kids than you?"

I challenged him to get out from under his burden of guilt and to begin to use the wisdom he had gained. If Christ could forgive prostitutes, surely He had forgiven this young man. "Go," I implored him. "Not only 'go and sin no more,' but also go and use your past as a tool. It can be immensely helpful to you as you try to share the anxieties of other people."

Immediately, my young friend felt a surge of release. After years of nagging guilt, he was washed clean in an act of sharing. Just as importantly, we had bathed with each other. He knew me and I knew him. And we loved and accepted each other for what we were and could become.

The psalmist recognized the value of being known. "Search me,

O God, and know my heart," he said. He also talked about "truth in the inward being."

You see, most of our religious problems are neither intellectual nor conceptual; they are relational. We desperately need to reach out and touch someone and have them reach out and touch us. Humans can't relate to one another if they look upon each other as robots. To mean something to each other, we have to relate as real, living, breathing, sweating, sobbing, laughing persons. We have to communicate from the depths of our real beings. If people today need anything, they need to be reassured that they have a personal worth and meaning which transcends the whirl of events in which they are engaged.

Many persons never get to know the joy of dancing at their funerals because they have psyched themselves into thinking they must always be powerful and even invulnerable. They fear that if they should level with themselves and reveal themselves to others, they may be crushed. And they intend to *crush,* not to *be crushed!*

In a cartoon, Satan is having a confab, a sort of sales meeting, with his devilish staff. "We've simply got to try harder," Satan says, "we're still Number Two." While apologizing to the car rental people and acknowledging that we must try harder, I must decry our popular but false stance of presuming that we can do anything if we'll just try a little harder. This process leads to a dead end.

Attempts to convey an image of strength and power feed on themselves and grow into ever-enlarging junkheaps of bankrupt relationships. We simply can't live up to the inflated images that we have created; in desperation, we build even bigger images which are even more difficult to protect. We frantically erect fences to hide our failures and our chagrin. Meanwhile, our innermost longing is to shuck off our pinching patent-leather shoes and slip into comfortable, well-worn loafers—to relax and be ourselves.

Let's face it, we're not
 as powerful as we've led people to believe,
 always calm and in control of our emotions,
 towers of strength,
 undefiled paragons of virtue.

Yet we continue our masquerade of pretense, pulling out all our
trump cards of power—playing these cards and hoping that the game
of relationship will end before we have to play our off-suit.

As I began measuring my own life against the formula I had
discovered—living depends on loving, loving depends on knowing,
knowing depends on risking—I found myself deficient. I had spun
about myself a shell. I couldn't afford to crack that shell wide enough
for even my wife to peek in.

But it became clear to me that Jerry couldn't love me deeply if
I didn't *need* her love, and not only *need* it, but let her *know* I
needed it. If I were the self-sufficient fellow I pretended, how could
I possibly need her?

There was only one suitable course of action, and I began to pursue
it. Gradually (at times painfully), I let Jerry in on my well-kept
secret: There remained inside me a cringing little country boy who
had ventured out into the world only to discover how economically,
socially, and intellectually deprived he had been, and who, fearing
that his inadequacies would show through, had frantically begun to
swath himself in roll after roll of protective shroud.

I was overjoyed when I discovered that Jerry could love the whole,
real me! Again, I experienced a resurrection.

Strangely, the enrichment of my relationship with Jerry came *after*
I had learned to be honest with a couple of professional associates.
But it was my new relationship with Jerry which persuaded me that
I could be honest with anyone, even strangers.

But what about those distressed people who came to me for counseling? Could I afford to reveal my weaknesses to them? Many came
to me because I was an authority figure—a real pro, they
thought—who could dish out specific solutions to specific problems.

I made a discovery—and it, too, had its painful aspects. Those people
hadn't really come to *listen* to me, they came for *me* to listen. I
became honest enough to recognize that most of those who went
away healed had, by and large, found healing within themselves
through a process of laying out their problem, analyzing it logically,
reviewing the options, and making a decision. My role had been to
keep them honest (my honest sharing did that) and to keep them
at their task until it was completed.

My counseling became a two-way street. I could let people know
that I, too, had problems with which I was wrestling. I could tell

them about approaches I had found helpful and about those that didn't work. Most of all, I could commiserate and let them know that I knew it was tough!

At this point, I committed myself to a ministry of relationship. In the past I had lectured people and pumped them up with unsolicited information. I had even told them how I had *won the victory!* Now I could simply lay my soul up against their souls; I could feel with them; I could let them come into my life and I could seek my way into theirs. The result: People found hope. They discovered that with God's help they could find within themselves sufficient resources to solve most of their problems.

How eager people are to have someone listen became dramatically apparent to me on a flight from Los Angeles to Baltimore. When we were about 30 minutes out of Baltimore, I made my way back to the rest room. It was occupied and I took a nearby seat.

I found myself next to a portly, well-dressed, obviously successful man. Just as obvious was his fatigue. I don't recall what started our conversation—maybe I said I'd be glad when we arrived in Baltimore. But he began telling his story and I became so interested that I forgot all about that little room back of us.

He was an oil company executive and was ripe for a vice-presidency, which would mean moving his family from Baltimore to Houston. He had been in Atlanta for five days, entertaining sales people on a merry-go-round of boozing and partying. Then, on Friday, he'd got a call ordering him to L.A., where he was to straighten out a distributor who was getting out of line. Now, at last, he was headed home.

"If you don't accept promotions when they're offered," he complained, "your superiors write you off. So you take them. But moving makes for a hard life. My wife and I have no friends in Baltimore; we figured we'd be here too short a time. If you put down roots, it's painful when you pull them up."

How long had they lived in Baltimore?

"Six years."

Six years! That's hardly temporary!

"What's it worth?" he implored. "You rise in the company, travel over the world, make a lot of money. But you come to retirement and find you have no place to call home and no friends to enjoy."

Our eardrums told us we were coming down. The executive gripped my hand and said, "I hadn't meant to burden you with my problems, but thank you for being so helpful."

Helpful? I hadn't said a hundred words. Mostly, I had nodded appreciatively.

This man's appearance was that of a powerful, successful, secure person. A big man. But inside, he and I were exactly alike. Inside him was a little boy, running scared and needing a friendly ear.

I wished him well, thanked him for sharing with me, told him he would have my prayers. And so we parted, never to see each other again. A stranger's lonely soul had rubbed against mine in meaningful encounter.

It was fortunate, what with the little bit of time that was available to us, that I hadn't become aware he was doing all the talking. He had told me all about himself, but I hadn't been able to tell him who I was. If I had sensed this omission, I might have been inclined to shout, "Hey, it's my turn! Let me tell you about me!"

What if I had told him I was a preacher? Would that have cut him off?

You aren't likely to cut someone off by telling them who you *really* are. *The Reverend Maxie D. Dunnam, holder of degrees, father confessor, knower of all things?* Sure, that would have shut him up. But I could have told him who I *really* am! I could have shared with him my own little-boy feelings.

I could have told him that as a minister, I move more often than most business executives do. I know the pain of pulling up roots once you've planted them.

I could have told him how drained I feel when I'm called upon to entertain people I don't enjoy or admire, and how much more draining it is to have somebody call at midnight and invite you to talk them out of suicide.

I could have told him about fears and disappointments I've experienced over promotions, salaries, and bosses. (And how many bosses I have had!)

I could have told him that I have suffered hurts, fears, and anxieties—in spite of being, and because of being, a minister.

But mostly I regret not having the opportunity to tell my new friend how supportive my faith in God and my sharing relationships with some close friends had been. I could have confessed to my friend that without the help of God and my friends, I would not have been able to move from death to resurrection.

I have become able to shift away from my old approach to life: viewing life as a continuously competitive battle. But occasionally I still find myself gearing up for battle—sharpening my words and patching my ecclesiastical armor, getting ready for the kill. However, through my resurrection, I've learned that these battles are *losing* battles and any victories that they produce are *hollow* victories. It is immensely more productive, and incomparably sweeter, to know and be known!

The psalmist knew that God knew him, every whit of him—and yet God loved him! What a breakthrough!

The psalmist was ahead of his time. In the New Testament we discover the great good news that even the Law of Love, "You shall love the Lord your God with all your heart, and with all your soul, and with all your mind . . . And you shall love your neighbor as yourself" (Matt. 22:37, 39 RSV) must be fulfilled in a relationship of gracious acceptance.

We are commanded to love, yet this condemns us. Who can fulfill that commandment? So we are miserably lost. But Christ fulfills the Law of Love and more. Through him we learn that God meets us where we are, in spite of our failures, in spite of our missing the mark of his creative intention for us. In Christ, God reconciles us to himself.

Paul could say, "God sent forth his Son . . . born under the law, to redeem those who were under the law" (Gal. 4:4-5 RSV). But here is the good news: *Not that we love God, but that he loved us and gave himself for us.* Known by God, we are still loved and accepted. That's cause to dance!

In the same category is the experience of letting another human know us. When we are able to throw off the paralyzing fear of being "found out," we can share with others. And lo! to our surprise and joy, we experience the love and acceptance of the person with whom we have risked our life in openness! Nothing exceeds that.

The "knowing" formula remains as exciting to me as it was that morning when it came to me as I walked along the sidewalk:

Living depends on loving,
loving depends on knowing,
knowing depends on risking.

The complete joy that comes with knowing and being known and
the freedom that knowing affords are worth any risk that may be
required.

Accepting the past. Knowing and being known. These are steps
away from death and toward resurrection.

Chapter 3

I Believe in Life After Birth!

It was strange. Here I was at a funeral and I wanted to dance. So I did. Oh, I didn't dance in the sense of shuffling my feet, but the dancing that I did in my mind and soul was every bit as real!

We were gathered to say goodbye to a friend who had died at age 72. His life had been so rich that we were able, on this occasion, to do something that we often pretend to do but cannot: We *celebrated* his life and memory. We rejoiced over the sharing that had been ours.

> He had gone full circle.
> A grey-haired man
>   who could hug another man
>   as freely as he could when he was only ten
>   because he had discovered
>   the meaning of love.

29

A time-sculptured face
    whose deep wrinkles
    provided natural channels
    thru which tears could flow unashamedly
    when touched by another's tenderness.

An innocent questioning about the future
    about life
    about hope
    because he wasn't
    long with us.

A quiet confidence
    that could confess a dependence
    upon God and others
    that didn't make him
    less than a man.

A bubbling up of life
    seen in his eyes
    his smile
    his warm concern
    present even in the face of death.

Our friend had made an important discovery. It had come too late in his life to suit him, but it would make great differences in our lives if we would only let it. His discovery: *There is life after birth.* At most funerals, those who attend focus on the question, "Is there life after *death?*" Here we engaged in an affirmation: "There is life after *birth.*"

I first ran across this seemingly turned-about expression at Fisherman's Wharf in San Francisco. My eleven-year-old daughter, Kim, was captivated by the buttons that were sold on every corner. They bore literally thousands of different signs, symbols, and slogans. Kim purchased one for me. She figured she had chosen one that was just right for a minister, and she was gleeful when she handed it to me. Its wording was: "Is there a life after birth?" Simple. Rather funny. But then not so simple. Rather serious! Probing!

I fastened the button onto my jacket—just to be a good sport, you know. But inwardly I knew that Kim, for all her innocence, had really nailed her dad! This was a most appropriate badge for me to wear. How many times had I asked, "Is there a life after birth?" Not in those words, but in the same vein.

Have you ever felt the numbness that comes upon finding no life in living? Have you ever looked back and wished you could live your life all over again? I have, more times than I can count.

It was one of those fleeting moments that are packed with meaning. I was returning to the church from lunch and he was departing following a noontime church event. Ordinarily, we would have exchanged routine greetings in passing, but on this occasion, a floodgate opened and the pure waters of soul-communication gushed out. Right there in the parking lot! It was one of those rare times when a person plunges to the core of things immediately—a moment of transparency which reveals the deeper concerns of one's life.

Even though he had a family to support, this young man had completed his college education. Now, at graduation time, he should have felt gratified and exhilarated; instead, he felt empty and listless.

But he expressed a hope, and this is what we talked about. In our worship, we have a period called "The Concerns and Celebrations of the Community." It's a sharing time when persons can bring their concerns so that we can be with them in prayer or otherwise exercise our ministry of caring, or they can tell of some good thing that has happened, some joy, in which case we can celebrate with them. The previous day, a mutual friend had revealed that he had found a new life, and we had celebrated with him. My young friend wanted new life, too, and he wanted me to help him find it.

I know persons who have spent a lifetime trying to find the courage to profess before some fellow human a commitment to new life. The time or the place never seems right. Yet, this young man had laid bare his soul in a parking lot! In clear and direct language and without any guise, he had committed himself to a new life in Christ.

Don't think that this kind of honesty and straightforwardness doesn't challenge a minister! While I rejoiced at my young friend's confession and rededication, I envied his ability to be that honest and free of pretention. I had longed to free myself of the burdens of the past, but the past had lain across my path like a fallen great tree. I had longed to know people and have them know me, but there was too much that I hated to reveal. I had wanted new life, but I was too entrenched in my old life to let go of it.

Now this young man had ministered to his minister. He had challenged me with his witness and had encouraged me with his determination. I left that parking lot praying, and later I filled out and clarified my prayer.

Lord, I have cheaply used what you have given me
I have held in my hands high and holy opportunities
    only to carelessly use them
    and cast them onto the dung heap
    of squandered hope.

In blind haste, I hurried through days
    that were pregnant with possibility,
    failing to "turn aside and see"
    what significant contribution I could make.

Those days were darkened
    by my shoddy labor,
    my calloused indifference,
    my cold insensitivity.

And Lord, I trod on the hopes and dreams of another,
    I poured the acid of my contempt on her,
    I may have irreparably damaged her budding soul.
Sin of Sins, Lord:
    I handled the pearls of your grace and love
        with dirty and clumsy fingers

I stood on your holy ground
    with desolately arid soul,
        unaware of your presence.

In my brash arrogance and smug pride,
    I stuck out my chest of self-assertion
        and said, "No!"

No, No, No!
And so I ordered my life on my own terms,
    and I lived my life in my own way.
Forgive me, Lord!

We know about remorse and death. But do we know about hope and life?

Well, let me tell you, what excites me these days is *life!*

I've been reading the Bible many years—15 as a preacher and, before that, spasmodically as a Sunday school student and as a college student who was interested in assembling artillery for intellectual engagements. But only recently have I discovered (and I'm amazed that I ever missed it) that resurrection is to be found on almost every page of the Bible. It's all brought together succinctly in Paul's shout: "When anyone is joined to Christ he is a new being: the old is gone, the new has come." (II Cor. 5:17 TEV)

All those years since my youth, I had been demanding a chance to start over. But that's impossible! And unimportant. The fact that you *can't* start over is only part of the essential truth: The encouraging and redeeming part is that you *don't need* to start over. The need is to start today—right now—living a new life. The past can't be blotted out, but we don't have to be shackled by it. That's the essence of the good news.

Nicodemus is one of the most fascinating men in the New Testament. I identify with him. Nicodemus came to Jesus by night to learn how he could shuck the drabness of his life and find new zest, but he deferred this urgent question, engaging instead in some polite talk about how great a teacher Jesus was. Jesus cut right to the point: "You must be born again!" This cryptic statement caused Nicodemus greater anguish. As if acting in behalf of all of us doubters, he implored: "How can a grown man be born again?" (John 3:4 TEV).

At birth, there is new life. *Sure.* But later? *Impossible!* We can't break out of the entanglements of lifetime habits. We can't climb out of ruts of character that have been cut by streams of deliberate decisions. We say, "Sow a thought and you reap an act. Sow an act and you reap a habit. Sow a habit and you reap a character. Sow a character and you reap a destiny."

And so we conclude: We *are* what we have made of life. What has been shaped and then baked in the kiln of time cannot be altered. What is written is written and cannot be blotted out or rewritten. The walls that we have built cannot be battered down. We are prisoners; there is no hope.

The reason that I identify with Nicodemus is that he knew what he wanted—a new life—but he was either unable or unwilling to pursue it.

"You must be born again."

"How can a man be born when he is old? Can he enter a second time into his mother's womb and be born?"

"You must be born of water and the spirit."

"Look, teacher, I know that some kind of radical change is necessary. You don't have to convince me of that. But this being born again is something that my experience tells me is impossible. Man, surely you don't mean to stand there and tell me that a full-grown guy like me can climb back up into his mother's womb and come back out again?"

Nicodemus wasn't questioning the *desirability* of change; he was questioning the *possibility* of change.

Now, 2000 years later, we're still talking about the possibility of change. We're talking about the possibility of dancing at our funeral. We modern Nicodemuses are saying, "Don't talk to me about the desirability of change; tell me it's possible, and how." We want to know

WHAT HAPPENS TO LIFE

Does it grow stale
    like week-old bread
    left unwrapped
Does it wilt
    like cut flowers

Does it dry up
    like a river bed
    in the heat of
    the summer sun
    or like the winter snow
    with the coming spring

Is it life or death
    to which we
    stumblingly move
    or both

Is it
     death after life
     or
     life after death
     or
     life after birth

If you'll stick with the story of Nicodemus, you may find an answer.
I did.

Nicodemus wanted new life. He was in spiritual pain and he wanted
to be healed. One is almost irritated at Jesus' response. Despite his
characteristic patience, Jesus seems taken back by the slowness of
Nicodemus' perception.

When Nicodemus presses the question, "How can a man be born
when he is old?" the answer that Jesus gives doesn't seem to be
an answer at all: "Truly, truly I say to you, unless one is born of
water and the spirit, he cannot enter the kingdom of God. That which
is born of flesh is flesh, and that which is born of spirit is spirit.
Do not marvel that I say unto you, you must be born anew."

Then, to add to Nicodemus' confusion, Jesus begins to talk about
the wind: "The wind blows where it wills, and you may hear the
sound of it, but you don't know from whence it comes or whither
it goes; so it is of everyone who is born of the spirit."

Do not marvel? How can one keep from marveling at this seeming
double-talk? Here is a man anguishing over his life and Jesus seems
to be turning him off. It's as though Jesus were saying, "Keep on
struggling, boy. You ought to be able to understand what I'm saying,
but if you don't, tough! And, really, you can't do much about your
situation anyhow, not unless the wind blows the right way."

For years I evaded that story because it made me angry with Jesus.
And now I know why it made me angry. I was so accustomed to
managing my own affairs that it was a put-down to have Jesus say
I couldn't manipulate my Christian experience. I wanted to manage
the Spirit the same way that I managed everybody and everything
else. I had credentials in theology and church organization, and I
wanted to systematize the work of God. In the personal area, I felt
quite capable of molding my own channel for the Spirit to flow
through, and I would let it flow in *my* chosen way and at *my* chosen
time.

But when I got to wrestling in earnest with my past and my
inability to know and be known, I went back and listened to what
Jesus was saying to Nicodemus—and to me:

"You want to be lord and master over the Spirit? *It'll never happen.*
The Spirit is unpredictable, mysterious, divine. Let me tell you about
something that you can better understand, although you can't see
it, at that. The wind. The wind blows; it cools, refreshes, invigo-

rates—and then it's gone. How? You don't know. Where does it come from and where does it go? You don't know.

"That's the way it is with the Spirit. He breaks in upon your dull lives at unexpected times. He cools, refreshes, invigorates. You begin to breathe, throw open the doors and windows of your being, lift your heads. Then—like the wind—the Spirit goes. It's a mystery and you've got to accept it as a mystery. You must not attempt to bring it under your mastery."

There, then, was the nub of my problem. I had mistakenly wanted a formula: One—two—three—and it would happen. Everything would be settled and I'd *have* my Christian experience. I could put it in a bag or box and keep it forever.

You can put it down that when you encounter someone who thinks he has a bag or box full of Christian experience, you'll find him to be a dull companion and a bore. Worse, he's dangerous! He offers a very limited package.

Jesus never gave us a one, two, three. Travail is as much a part of spiritual birth as is physical birth.

You may say to me, "Hold on! Maxie. You take off after people who claim to have a formula for getting Christian experience in a bag or box. Yet, you're putting your formula into a book. What gives?"

I hear you. It took me months to decide to write this book because I didn't want to come off as one offering pat answers, and if that's what you're feeling, I've failed. This is not my intention.

Writing a book is, in a sense, a presumption. It's presumptious to assume you have something of value to share with others. But, in a sense, I had no choice. I am compelled to share what it's like to have the cleansing and refreshing winds of the Spirit whistle through my hollow, arid being, bringing relief, renewal, *resurrection*. And I believe that if I, with all that I had going against me, can learn to dance, there's universal hope.

Is there life after birth? Yes! In bulbs and buds—in babies grown old! The old man that we had come to bury was a testament to the things I've tried to recapture in this chapter. He was a man old in calendar years, but he had about him the freshness of a child! He had been reborn, again and again. And at his funeral, I was so overcome by the undying quality of his life that I wanted to dance! Maybe T. S. Eliot was right:

> What we call the beginning
> is often the end and to make an end
> is to make a beginning.
> The end is where we start from.

And the end where we start is the celebration of an assurance that *there is life after birth!*

"Although you were dead . . . he (God) has made you alive with Christ . . ." (Col. 2:13 NEB)

I can't *give you a formula* for a new aliveness, I can only *share with you my experience.* I've discovered that there is a beginning which is common to every experience, no matter what has gone before. This beginning is the point of decisiveness where we turn to God with a new attentiveness—a new openness to his possibilities. This beginning is the time when we wrestle with the "Yes" and "No" of our lives. (Not just in some part of our lives, but in the whole of our lives.) We begin anew when we say "Yes."

To say "Yes" is the ultimate act of the will. It is beyond the level of feeling and emotion, although feeling and emotion are involved. To say "Yes" is to surrender.

Surrender? Our red flags go up! We don't like that word, even in a religious context. This amazes me, because surrender is a vital part of our lives. Many psychiatrists and psychologists are recommending surrender. The great Swiss psychiatrist Paul Tournier wrote a book called *Surrender* in which he contends that a willingness to

Like the wind, the Spirit comes and goes, and we know not how.

surrender is the pivotal point for becoming a whole person. Alan Watts, who has turned to the submissive life-flow of Zen and other Eastern philosophies, says, "Faith is no misconception. It is a plunge into the unknown. Belief *clings* but faith *lets go.*" (Italics mine.)

Freedom through surrender seems a paradox, but it should not appear so strange to us. Death and resurrection are written into the whole scheme of nature and life. In the autumn, the tree casts its golden leaves into the wind, and it dies for the winter. In the spring, a new miracle, the miracle of life, takes place. The tree dresses out in new leaves; tender buds blossom; there is fruit. All this testifies to the miracle of "life after birth." And the end is—no, the *beginning* is: *There is life after birth!*

The wind of the Spirit can tousle, tease, refresh, rattle, sting, startle. It can knock you down. It knocked me down. And I'm glad that it did! If it hadn't, I might have missed the key to it all: *There is life after birth!*

there is life after birth

Chapter 4

Real at Last

Earl Loomis in "The Self In Pilgrimage" tells of a little boy who was sitting at a lunch counter with his mother and older sister. After taking the mother's and sister's orders, the waitress addressed Little Brother. "What will you have, young man?"

"*I'll* order for him," said the sister.

Again the waitress asked the boy what he would have, and the mother said, "*I'll* order for him."

The waitress repeated, "Young man, what will you have?"

"A hamburger," the youngster said.

"Would you like it rare, medium, or well done?"

"Well done, please," said the lad, brightening a bit.

"Would you like mustard, pickles, onions, relish, or ketchup?"

In a burst of self-confidence, the boy exclaimed, "The whole works!"

As the waitress walked away, the lad said, "Gee, Mommy, she thinks I am real."

To be real. How does it feel? It feels great! Being real even makes a hamburger taste better.

Real life is the kind of life that Jesus promised: "I came that they may have life, and have it abundantly" (John 10:10 KJV). This new life with new freedom is for me the *resurrection* life. The secularist might call new life "turning over a new leaf." A fundamentalist might call it *salvation,* a great word meaning "wholeness" but too often limited to something hoped for after death. Some call new life *being born again,* which again is a fine expression capable of meaning "turning around and taking a new direction," but which is crippled if made dependent upon a rigid set of beliefs. Some call new life *conversion,* which captures the sense of change and growth so long as we don't reduce it to a dogmatic formula.

Whatever we call it, new life didn't come handily for me.

In the *Velveteen Rabbit,* Margery Williams captures the essence of what I'm talking about with disarming simplicity.

The Rabbit, who was made of velveteen and stuffed with sawdust, felt very ordinary among the fancier toys of the Boy's nursery; indeed, only the Skin Horse was kind to him.

The Skin Horse had lived longer in the nursery than any of the others. He was so old that his brown coat was bald in patches and showed the seams underneath, and most of the hairs in his tail had been pulled out to string bead necklaces. He was wise, for he had seen a long succession of mechanical toys, and would never turn into anything else. For nursery magic is very strange and wonderful, and only those playthings that are old and wise and experienced like the Skin Horse understand all about it.

"What is REAL?" asked the Rabbit one day, when they were lying side by side near the nursery fender, before Nana came to tidy the room. "Does it mean having things that buzz inside you and a stick-out handle?"

"Real isn't how you are made," said the Skin Horse. "It's a thing that happens to you. When a child loves you for a long, long time, not just to play with, but REALLY loves you, then you become Real."

"Does it hurt?" asked the Rabbit.

"Sometimes," said the Skin Horse, for he was always truthful. "When you are Real you don't mind being hurt."

"Does it happen all at once, like being wound up," he asked, "or bit by bit?"

"It doesn't happen all at once," said the Skin Horse. "You become. It takes a long time. That's why it doesn't often happen to people who break easily, or have sharp edges, or who have to be carefully kept. Generally, by the time you are Real, most of your hair has been loved off, and your eyes drop out and you get loose in the joints and very shabby. But these things don't matter at all, because once you are Real you can't be ugly, except to people who don't understand."

"I suppose *you* are Real?" asked the Rabbit. And then he wished he had not said it, for he thought the Skin Horse might be sensitive. But the Skin Horse only smiled.

"The Boy's uncle made me Real," he said. "That was a great many years ago but once you are Real, you can't become unreal again. It lasts for always."

Eventually, the Rabbit *did* become Real. He knew it when one day he had been left out in the yard after a long day of play with the little boy. Nana, the nurse, had to find him and bring him to the boy in bed before the boy would go to sleep. "Fancy all that fuss for a toy!" she said. The Boy sat up in bed and reached out for the Rabbit. "Give me my Bunny! You mustn't say that. He isn't a toy. He's REAL."

When the little Rabbit heard that, he was very happy, for he knew that what the Skin Horse had said was true at last. The nursery magic had happened to him, and he was no longer a toy. He was REAL. The boy himself had said it.

Sometimes, in order for us to grasp an obvious truth, we have to throw the clutch and shift our minds out of "literal" gear into "intuitive" gear. This "children's story" (calling it that gives us adults an excuse to read it) is so devastatingly simple that its truth comes through without effort. The truth is: *Real* life is set in relationships. I think this was what Jesus was talking about when he said, "I came that they may have life, and have it abundantly (John 10:10 RSV). He came that you may have a life of relationship. And that is what Paul meant when he wrote to the Ephesians, "God's mercy is so abundant, and his love for us is so great, that while we were spiritually dead . . . he brought us to life with Christ" (Eph. 2:4 TEV).

The hunger to be real is universal and intense. This brings a "hospital" joke to mind.

One fellow said to the other, "I had an operation and the doctor left a sponge inside."

"Do you experience pain?"

"No, but I sure get thirsty!"

There's something deep within me that causes me to thirst for real life. I can't tell you precisely what this thirst-generating mechanism is, but let me try. (I can assure you it isn't a sponge!)

One basic part of this something-deep-inside-me apparatus is a monitor which indicates quite reliably when I'm "alive" and when I'm "not alive."

The "print-out" is in words like these:

"I was not myself."

"I don't know why I did it—it was so unlike me."

"I feel that something is missing."

"Is this all there is?"

When I get readings like these, I now know it's time to seek real life.

Thirst for real life is acknowledged time and again in the Bible. And the Bible also tells us how this thirst can be satisfied.

A theme which echoes through the Old Testament is, "I have set before you life and death . . . therefore choose life" (Deut. 30:19 RSV). Here "life" and "death" don't signify "existence" and "nonexistence;" rather, they hold a promise that existence can be enriched and thereby become real life. You can have either a *dead* life or a *real* life—one that is lived in confidence, hope, and gratitude. This promise is capable of fulfillment within one's lifetime.

The offer of life was made first to a people, Israel. Later, the same offer was extended to individuals, but it was clearly stated that real life could come to an individual only through a covenant with God and a community with other persons.

The offer of life is also central in the New Testament. For example, Paul says to the Ephesians, "God's mercy is so abundant, and his love for us is so great, that while we were spiritually dead he brought us to life with Christ" (Eph. 2:4 TEV). Again, John's Gospel explains that Jesus came to abolish death and to open the possibility of abundant life to all men. I think that "death" here speaks of a weakness or a nulling of the life-experience rather than any ceasing to exist. "Life," on the other hand, suggests a higher state of existence. This higher state, this aliveness, is available only through God.

The New Testament proclaims that Jesus possesses the real life for which men thirst and he has the unique power to communicate this life to us. "In him was life; and the life was the light of men" (John 1:4 KJV). And, "I came that they may have life, and have it abundantly" (John 10:10 KJV).

"REAL isn't how you are made," said the Skin Horse, "it's something that happens to you."

The real life which Jesus offers is not some special kind of "religious" or "spiritual" life in contrast to life in the world. This real life isn't attained by putting ourselves on a shelf where we will be protected from contamination. We find this life in fellowship with God and fellow humans.

It's no wonder that our traditional connotation of "eternal life" hasn't grabbed young people. The young person (and some of us who aren't so young) is more interested in the possibilities of living a "now" life. And if he misinterprets the New Testament message to be talking about new life way out there somewhere, it's our fault. "Eternal life" is life having a quality that is beyond the reach of death. Jesus said, "This is eternal life: to know thee who alone art truly God, and Jesus Christ whom thou hast sent" (John 17:3 NEB).

We kill the soul of the gospel and deaden the dynamic of the Spirit-life when we confuse Christianity with the decent, safe, and comfortable life which the church sometimes mistakenly labels "Christian." Too many children are brought up in a sterile Christianity-culture which causes them to assume that the so-called "religious" people about them are actually living the Jesus Life which the New Testament promises. We ought to be honest and tell the kids that what they see is middle-class morality tied up with a ribbon of mistaken piety.

No wonder people are turned off when we try to sell them a life that is akin to death. What we really have to offer is a stupendous attraction and we should dare to share it as the revolutionary, head-turning, heart-warming, life-heaving thing that it is.

"God's mercy is so abundant, and his love for us is so great, that while we were spiritually dead . . . he brought us to life with Christ."

We can't squint at such a promise—
    Eyes open!
We can't shuffle along this path,
    somersaults are in order!
This is no quiet matter for chamber conversation:
    Bring on the megaphone for shouting.
The words are bouncy:
    free
    bold
    flying
    high
    tingling
    enveloping
    rippling
    blowing
    laughing
    hoping

This life is not a dream for dying man
    but resurrection for dead-men now.

A leap and a laugh.
A spin and a swirl.
A celebration and a song.
Not a dream for dying men,
    a dance for *living* ones.

    Life is more than a word; it is an experience. The work of God through Christ in our lives is the work of *life*—the work of making us *real*. Certain words leap out at me as I read the New Testament.

"I came that they may have life, and have it abundantly"
(Jn. 10:10 RSV).

"To all who received him, . . . he gave power to become . . ."
(Jn. 1:12 RSV).

"If any one is in Christ, he is a new creation . . ." (II Cor. 5:17
RSV).

"But God's mercy is so abundant, and his love for us so great,
that while we were spiritually dead . . . he brought us to
life with Christ . . ." (Eph. 2:4 TEV).

"For it is by God's grace that you have been saved, through
faith. It is not your own doing, but God's gift" (Eph. 2:8
TEV).

We could go on citing Scripture, but what does it all add up to?
What does *abundant life* mean to me? It means being able to accept
and utilize my past. It means being able to reveal myself to other
persons and to appreciate what I see in them. It means being able
to celebrate life after birth. We've talked about these stages in my
growth experience in past chapters. Add to these elements the dimension that I have introduced in this chapter: Abundant life is (again,
I hesitate because of the way these words are so often distorted)
"being saved."

Being saved
from the stifling kind of fear
that the life-miracle
would never happen to me;
that I would never make it,
either in this world
or any other.
Being saved
from a guilt
that gnawed my soul away
when I failed to perform
or meet the expectations
others placed upon me,
or the expectation I thought
God was laying upon me.
Being saved
from a groveling self-pity,
that buried myself
in myself.
Being saved
from the tenacious bonds
of works-righteousness,
the deep drive
to *be* right
and *do* right
in order that God and my friends
might count me worthy.
Being saved
from sin
life centered in self,
locked-in living.
From all this,
yes, and more, much more.
Being saved to life.
Liberated,
Released from the shackles of proving,
and dancing
in the joy of being.

Released from the fetters of hostility and hatred
 and relishing in the shared life
 of open and honest relationships.
Released from emptiness and futility
 and feeling the joy
 of investing my life
 in other lives.

Behold I Am Doing A New Thing

Not *all* the time—oh, no! Not all the time, but enough times to feel the joy of being alive and real. Being carefree—not indifferent, but *carefree*. (There's a difference.) Not bound to illegitimate preconceptions; not tied to the hell of predictability and playing it safe; not having to "hop to" because someone lays something on me. Being liberated from my tied-up, cautious, ungiving self. Liberated to dance as the self that God intended me to be when I was born. *Being saved*—living in grace: that unlimited, unmerited love of God that frees me!

No, not all the time, but enough of the time to know what the Velveteen Rabbit knew when the Boy pronounced him real. The life that Christ gives us is real, and to get a taste of it (and that's about all I've gotten, a taste) makes me want more of it for myself and for you.

"Real isn't how you are made," said the Skin Horse, "it's something that happens to you."

"God's mercy is so abundant, and his love for us is so great," said Paul, "that while we were spiritually dead he brought us to life with Christ."

"I came that you may have life," said Jesus, "and have it abundantly."

"It doesn't happen all at once," said the Skin Horse. "You become." Yes, wise old Skin Horse, that's so in nursery magic. But in the grace of God's life-miracle, *becoming* can begin now. "For it is by God's grace that you have been saved, through faith. It is not your own doing, but God's gift" (Eph. 2:8 TEV).

We can receive the gift of life now, and begin the process of becoming REAL.

Not tomorrow—

But now!

Real life!

Born again life!

Resurrection!

Chapter 5

Getting
It All
Together

The experience of Specialist 4 Jacky C. Bayne was strange beyond belief.

Jacky, a soldier in Vietnam, was mangled by a booby trap. For 45 minutes, medics tried to revive him, then gave him up as dead. His seemingly lifeless body was shipped to a Graves Registration unit.

Sometime later—nobody knows how long—the embalmer's knife flicked the body and there was a quiver. Jacky was rushed to a field hospital. Given resuscitation and transfusions, he revived. Three veteran army doctors said they'd never seen anything like it.

Strange!

For some reason, I had clipped out of a newspaper an account of Jacky's experience. Now as I fingered the yellowed clipping, I felt that I understood, if only vaguely, something of the miracle of Jacky Bayne. Moreover, I felt a warm sense of kinship with him.

The clipping was dated Nov. 3, 1967, and I had run across it three years later. The article said Jacky was moving toward a limited recovery.

I felt compelled to learn what had happened to Jacky in the interim.

The clipping gave his hometown as Fort Mill, S.C. The telephone operator said there were six Baynes listed in Fort Mill, and I made a random choice. The Bayne that I got was an aunt. Yes, the aunt said, Jacky was alive. He was at that moment in the Veterans Hospital in Columbia, S.C., having surgery on an arm. I called the hospital and talked to Jacky, this "once-dead" stranger whose story had become so important to me.

Jacky appreciated my call. He told me about many things—his new home in Fort Mill, his father's death the previous year, his mother's eye surgery, his hopes of becoming able to use the arm and of learning to walk, and his activities in First Baptist Church.

"Jacky, how did you feel upon learning that you had come so close to being buried?"

"I was numb for a long time, but then I knew God was giving me life again."

Jacky was able to talk about life. He had been on his way to his funeral and had experienced a resurrection!

My thoughts jumped to another person in another time. A woman who had come to the well at Sychar in Samaria at noon rather than in the evening, when most of the women came. (In the evening, the air was cool and filled with choice gossip.) It happened that Jesus was at the well at the same time. How important this woman must have felt when Jesus initiated conversation and asked of her, "Give me a drink." Jesus' acknowledgement of her presence affirmed her as a person, which was her greatest need. But there was special meaning here, too. Jesus was a "have" and she was a "have-not."

"How can you, a Jew, ask for a drink from me, a woman of Samaria?" she asked.

Jesus responded, "If you knew what God can give, and if you knew who it is that said to you, 'Give me a drink', I think you would have asked him, and he would have given you living water!"

The woman was taken aback. She didn't understand. "Sir, you have nothing to draw with and the well is deep—where can you get your living water?"

"Everyone who drinks this water will be thirsty again. But whoever drinks the water I will give him will never be thirsty again. For my gift will become a spring in the man himself, welling up into eternal life."

Jesus' words puzzled her mind, but his authenticity appealed to her heart.

"Sir," she implored, "give me this water, so that I may stop being thirsty—and not have to draw water any more."

There is more to the story, which is related in John 4:1-30. The woman confessed her involvement with many men—but Jesus knew this already. He didn't condemn her as did the self-righteous women whom she evaded by coming to the well at midday. The story closes with the woman realizing that here was the one who had life to give. She was so overcome that she left her water jar behind and rushed into the town to shout, "Come see the man who told me everything I've ever done. Can this be the Christ?"

Jacky Bayne had been dead, but now he is alive. The woman at the well had been spiritually and socially dead, but she found new life. I can relate to these two persons. The three of us were headed to a funeral and wound up experiencing resurrection.

Life! There's no more significant word, is there? Jesus continually spoke of life. Often we don't act like it, but *life* is the tie that joins Jesus and us.

What does *life* look like? I'm not talking about the biological dimension of life that was rescued from the embalmer's knife. I'm thinking of something beyond the physiology of hearts pumping blood and lungs gulping air, as important as these functions are. I'm talking about the kind of life that begins when someone sees the contradiction between what he is and what he might become and decides he will do something to remedy his situation. I'm talking about the life-urge to say "I" and really mean it.

I want to say *I*
To say it
and mean it
But that's an awesome act

To say I is
to take responsibility
for my thoughts
my attitudes
my actions

To say I is
> to choose an identity
> to accept a name
> and a face
> to cease being an it

To say I is
> to be willing to be known
> to be accountable
> to respond to life
> to open myself
> > to the response of others

But that's an awesome act

To say I is
> to eliminate the possibility of hiding
> to end the practice of blaming others for me
> or to praise them for me

To say I
> is to be me
> all of me
> I want to . . .
> But that's an awesome act!

No doubt, you, too, have moments when you feel more genuinely "you" than at other times. At other times we say, "I was not myself." These are the times when we recognize, from the negative side of the fence, that there is a vast difference between the path of self-fulfillment and the ruts of a bland existence. Such moments are precious, for it is in them that we learn the life-style to which we are called.

Thank God there stirs within us an awareness of when we are "alive" and when we are "not alive." Thank God we occasionally recognize that our lives are hobbled by mediocrity.

But the urgent question is: How can we become free so that we can live released, vibrant, rewarding lives?

We all hunger for real life, but the responses vary from person to person and from time to time. Sometimes we reach out for life, as did the woman at the well. At other times, we deny our hunger, or else we quiet it by eating junk with "empty calories." Our junk includes acquisition of inanimate things, losing ourselves in a whirl of "busy" activities, shielding ourselves in the wrappings of social status.

Why do we refuse to listen to the beat of our own life-drum? Why do we, instead, go traipsing off behind the brass band of an anonymous crowd? Why do we refuse the invitation to be authentic?

The most publicized clash of our day is between the aliveness-seekers (mostly our youth), who dig vibrations of change, and the security-seekers (mostly adults), who resent and fear change. Each proposal for change must, of course, be judged on its merits. Either to clutch a given life-style because it is old or to seek out another life-style merely for the sake of newness is superficial and dangerous.

The Gospel writer said of Jesus' mission and purpose: "In him was life; and the life was the light of men" (Jn. 1:4 KJV). Paul, describing what happened when a person experiences Christ's gift, said, "If any one is in Christ, he is a new creation; the old has passed away, behold, the new has come" (II Cor. 5:17 RSV).

The woman at the well had become badly fractured in the tug-of-war between the "good" and "evil" forces in her life. Then she met Jesus. He healed her—he glued the parts back together and she went away whole.

What we're talking about here is *integrity*. One definition of integrity is "the state of being complete or undivided."

I certainly was not complete. I was a one-man war.

I used my deprived background as a rationalization to excuse my dividedness: If I wasn't successful, I had an excuse for my failure—even God wouldn't expect much out of a poor kid from Perry County, Mississippi!

While I didn't use this excuse often, it served as an ace in the hole. With it, I could explain away an occasional bad grade in college or seminary—my background was inadequate. I had a dreadful fear of failure, and this rationalization was always there to fall back on.

I cultivated the estrangement of my various selves, yet there was within me a surging desire to be whole. There was something within me that demanded that I acquire (or recover) integrity. To use the modern idiom, I knew that I had to "get it all together."

In adolescence, I started gathering up my deprivations and dumping them into a bag labeled "Poor Me." By the time I had reached young adulthood, I had accumulated quite a bundle of self-pity. As this bundle grew larger, my resentment and bitterness increased. The burden almost broke me.

Again, although I relished having this bag of excuses, I also wanted to rid myself of it. Perhaps wearing a magic "Christian" badge would chase away the gloom. It didn't. Well, even if being a "Christian" wouldn't give me *instant* relief, surely it would provide me "salvation" in the after-life. With this in mind I devoted myself to dogma. I would be *right* in my beliefs. This, too, turned out to be an empty exercise. There was no *now* relief to it, no *now* hope.

All along, I fed myself a black pill from my handy-dandy "Christian kit." This pill was *self-condemnation*. It was one of the primary prescriptions of my "brand" of Christianity at that time. Self was to be put down, to be negated, to be brought under subjection—not to be fulfilled, unified, made whole.

Rather than helping with a cure, the pill of self-condemnation only made matters worse.

At this point in my life, a psychologist friend introduced me to the work of Abraham Maslow. This was the "pill" I desperately needed.

In the past, psychologists believed that we could best understand psychological health by first understanding psychological illness. Maslow provided an alternative viewpoint. Instead of studying sick people, he studied healthy ones—those who had achieved a high degree of self-satisfaction or fulfillment. These were the "healthy champions"—the models of what people could be.

That made a lot of sense to me.

I noted that Jesus was one of the persons who, according to Maslow, demonstrated self-actualization. I started looking at Jesus in that light. I learned what Jesus was all about. He didn't come to tear me up and scatter the pieces. He came to help me to "get it all together." His purpose was to help me to find personhood and to celebrate it.

How had I missed the true meaning of the New Testament all those years? I had missed it because I had no facility for self-communication. I couldn't talk with myself—we weren't even on speaking terms!

I start the day numbly
  the coffee helps
  but the focus is still blurred.

"I can do all things
  through Christ who strengthens me!"

A pretty big order!

A dreamy possibility.

It takes courage
  to even get up
  to shake the creepies of fear.
I need to get it all together
  but is that a delusion
  . . . wishful thinking
  . . . an impossible task?

Bits and pieces of me are everywhere
  in last year's failure
  in yesterday's bungle
  in tomorrow's dreams
  bits and pieces are scattered everywhere.

Get it all together?

Endurance—
  I need that
    to face this day
      as best I can
    Moving on
      letting the chips
      fall where they may

Bits and pieces of me everywhere

Or gather
the bits and pieces together
Meeting the now with courage
and catching the future with hope.

But more than endurance.

Honesty and *self-assessment*
To know myself
as a weakling—
impotent to resist
as a giant
with untapped strength
as a mixture and a mess
a hero and a coward
a laugher and a crier
a talker and a listener
a reconciler and a fighter
a lover and a hater
To know the we in me.

Sometimes I relish me
At other times I can't tolerate me.
Sometimes I feel all in one piece
Sometimes as though I'm barely holding together

Integrity
getting it all together
the urges and impulses
the power and weakness
the forms and functions
of my life
man
husband
father
friend
minister
all together . . .
In one piece.

I've learned that I have many selves, including some negative selves. I seek to recognize and experience all of these selves so that they can have communication one with the other and thereby become integrated into my whole self. Self-pity, or self-condemnation, or self-rejection comes when I see one of my "little" selves as the whole me. If my greedy self emerges (as it often does) to drive me to seek "things" which I didn't have in childhood, I have to be careful not to see that as the entire me—likewise, when I am jealous, lustful, possessive, hateful. No one of these is my whole self. I am a kingdom of selves. Recognizing this, I am able to move toward wholeness.

The Hebrew word *Shalom* (which we translate as "Peace") is the experience of enjoying inner unity—the experience of enjoying being one. Our Peace is Christ. We put him at the center. No matter how much the circles of our lives enlarge and no matter how many selves we discover, we have a single, divine Center upon which everything converges.

With Christ holding us together, we become able to examine our many selves, cultivating the positive and utilizing even the negative. All the while, we enjoy an enormous sense of power and peace. Jesus said, "You will know the truth, and the truth shall make you free" (Jn. 8:32 RSV).

To say "Christ" is to say "unity," "wholeness." When we speak of "Christ within us," we are talking about bringing our many selves into a harmonious relationship around this divine Center. We're talking about *integrity!*

A second word which characterizes new life in Christ is *investment*. Integrity pulls our selves together. Through investment, the integrated self moves out to bring new life to all men.

Jesus said, "You shall love the Lord your God with all your heart, and with all your soul, and with all your mind" (Matt. 22:37 RSV). That's *integrity*. And "You shall love your neighbor as yourself" (Matt. 22:39 RSV). That's *investment*.

You can't have new life without investment. If you isolate yourself from other people, you'll find that you have insulated yourself from the source of power. Like the woman at the well, people around us are seeking renewal. You and I may be the only ones who can offer them the water jug of new life.

To be uninvolved is to be irresponsible. We let the well within us dry up. A reformed alcoholic recognizes that he can best preserve

Integrity

"You shall love the Lord your God with all your heart, mind, soul and strength...."

"...And you shall love your neighbor as yourself."

his newly acquired wholeness by investing his life in those who have yet to win the struggle.

In my city, there is a chapter of an organization called Fish. These people respond as good neighbors to the emergency needs of other persons. A call to an advertised phone number, day or night, brings help. A friend of mine, Louise, was chairman of Fish, and she received a call from a mother of seven children who was to have surgery the next day and would need someone to care for the children for a week.

Louise checked 30 or 40 volunteers without success. When Dan came home from work, Louise told him it looked as though they themselves were going to be taking care of seven children. Dan's comment was, "Okay, but if this is the work of the Lord, undoubtedly someone will respond."

At 11 that night, the phone rang. A young woman, Stephanie, was calling from a neighboring city. She had heard about the woman's need through her church's telephone counseling service. She was taking a week off from her job and she would spend it with the children.

Two weeks later, the steering committee of Fish called to invite Stephanie to their meeting. Sure, Stephanie said, she would be happy to come, but could Louise arrange transportation?

"Won't you be able to drive?"

"Oh," Stephanie said. "I thought you knew. I'm blind!"

Stephanie was also being treated for cancer of the larynx. ("Can you imagine me without a voice?" she asked cheerfully.)

Stephanie had put it all together! And she was investing herself.

After sharing the story of Stephanie with my congregation, I received a poem in the mail. Some person who chose to be anonymous wrote:

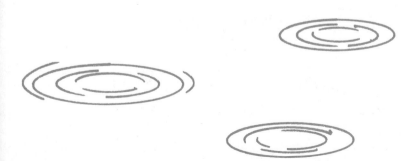

Like a flat, smooth rock I've skipped across
The waves of life—soar—dip—skim—soar again
And yet again, just tipping the water
Long enough to fly. But, somehow, Lord,
I know it's not the way you'd have me go.
I think you want a rugged, solid rock
That travels from your hand in graceful arc
And plummets down—clear down—into the depths
Where all the lovely dangers are of deep, green waters;
Where you feel the current's power surge
And, committed, find your strength in its embrace.
Wave-skippers never know that deep-down place!

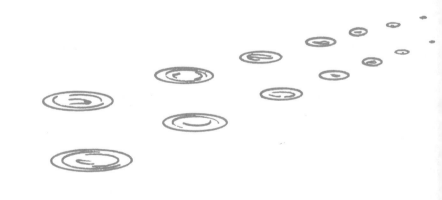

That's loving the Lord your God with all your heart, soul, and mind. That's *integrity!* It's also loving your neighbor as yourself. That's *investment!*

Take the scattered pieces of your life—the empty moments, the soul-hungerings, the conscience-gnawings, the yearnings and strivings. Recognize them and affirm them. Meld them with the more positive pieces of your life—the caring and sharing, singing and laughing, praising and dancing. Get it all together. Then invest it!

Like the fabled phoenix bird, from the ashes of what you used to be there will arise new life. And *that's* resurrection!

Chapter 6

Marriage: Ballroom for Dancing

The flower of love burst into full blossom and Jerry and I "became one" in marriage.

I didn't know it then, but the flower of love is a fragile thing, demanding a lot of attention. It must be watered with intentional honesty and fed with deliberate care, else it will fade and lose its fragrance. During the first half of our 15 years of marriage, I didn't give our flower that kind of attention.

At least once, I almost chopped this flower down. We had been married a few months and this was our first conflict. I wasn't prepared to recognize conflict, much less deal with it.

I had told myself that to become angry is bad, and to express anger is worse. I had convinced myself that "mature" people don't get upset—certainly they don't cry! Another illusion of mine: All ministers have *perfect* marriages; otherwise, they aren't worthy of their profession.

With my distorted professional image squeezing in, there was no chance for my personal image to emerge: Preachers don't lose their temper—I am a preacher—I don't lose my temper.

Jerry hadn't been "schooled" in this kind of control. She came from a family where love was shown in open physical expressions. Tears and laughter flowed freely. Hugging and kissing were common and feelings were honored.

I married her when she was only a year out of high school. She had not been exposed to preacher images or "preacher's wife" models. On this occasion she really expressed herself! I responded calmly, which upset her all the more. Soon she was crying.

"This," I said, "is outrageous."

My superior air made her feel like dirt.

I stalked out of the bedroom and went downstairs, calling over my shoulder, "When you're ready to discuss this calmly like an adult, I'll be in my study."

A big hunk of Jerry died that day, and a big hunk of our relationship died, too. I wasn't alive enough to sense the pain, but Jerry was and she felt it!

Five-five, with long blonde hair and soft blue eyes, Jerry stands out in a crowd. She's beautiful! Something about her, even today, is "little girlish." (When she answers the door, strangers sometimes ask, "Is your father at home?") There is a childlikeness about her in characteristics other than her physical appearance. She blushes easily, laughs and cries spontaneously, gets excited quickly, recounts episodes with a liveliness that enables you to experience what she has experienced, and is deeply sentimental. She's one of the most unaffected persons I know. Jerry is, well, *always Jerry*. She is honest and has a way of cutting through a lot of "stuff" to get at the core of things.

I failed to affirm all this in Jerry. Years later, I learned just how traumatic that bedroom experience had been, and how my failure to accept her as a feeling person had thwarted her personal growth. For years memories of that encounter shut down the free flow of her feelings. Depth communication was rare.

It's too bad that I didn't know then what I know now. From later experience and from counseling with others, I have learned something else, too: Marriages that have withered through neglect can be brought back to life again.

Few marriages are as effective as they ought to be. Most marriages are of the "garden variety." Sadly, couples either pretend satisfaction with their relationship (as mediocre as it may be), or they recognize that something is missing but can't get a handle on the problem.

As a result, they settle for a starvation diet when they could be feasting upon a banquet of joy and fulfillment. They could be dancing in a wonderful ballroom!

The first step toward recovery is to recognize that things aren't right. Let me share with you the anguish that I feel when things aren't right between Jerry and me:

Lord, I don't know what's going on.
Something happened.
Was it me?
Or her?
We were together, but now we're apart.

I feel that apartness.
We're together in marriage.
We act politely.
We speak calmly.
but what we say has little meaning.
We move without too much contact.
All this makes me aware of our apartness

We're not together as persons.
We smile
but we don't laugh.
We speak
but we don't share.
We touch
but we don't feel.
There's distance between us;
We're strangers now.
I don't like this, Lord.
I feel empty
lost
dead.

What am I afraid of?
    rejection
    that she doesn't feel what I feel
    that she is unaware of the chasm
    that the emptiness is only my own
    that the failure is mine?

Maybe I don't want to expose myself
    to honesty
    to hurt
    I don't want to admit failure
        to be vulnerable
        to be dependent on her response.

I need to move
    to decide
    to act.

I know this is love—
    to decide
        despite my feelings
        my aches
    to move
        despite my inertia
    to act
        despite my fear.
I will rise and go.

We don't need to know the cause;
    that we are separate
    is hell enough.

Help me, Lord,
    to move
    to decide
    to act.

Thank goodness I feel apartness only *some* of the time!

A teacher had her third-graders draw pictures of what they wanted to be when they grew up. They depicted firemen, doctors, actresses— you know, their usual choices. But one girl handed in a blank sheet of paper.

"Don't you know what you want to be?"

"Well—I want to be married, but I don't know how to draw it."

All too often, we don't have an adequate picture of marriage. In the next few pages, I'd like to share with you my mind's-eye-view of marriage. I'll sketch broad outlines and let you fill in the fine lines from your own experience. At the same time, let me caution you that marriage, like any relationship, is continuously changing. It's dynamic, therefore capable of growth (and, alas, *death*). The picture changes.

Married love looks like decision. Marriage is more than feeling; it's also intention.

You may protest that love is—well, love *is!* If you love somebody, you know it and you don't have to take your love apart to see what makes it tick.

There's truth in this dissent, but not the whole truth. The spontaneous love that we feel at the time we marry may lose some of its zest. Our feelings may become numb, causing our concept of marriage to become vague and confused. Then, down deep in that mysterious abyss of "ourselves," we begin to doubt: Am I in love? Was I *ever* in love?

Many people come to me expressing doubt. They even question whether it's right for them to go on living with a person for whom genuine *feelings* of love are missing. (At least we have to credit them with recognizing that a marriage license does not legitimize an estranged relationship.)

The shifting of our feelings makes *decision* an important aspect of marriage. These feelings must be understood and expressed. The feelings of courtship are different from the feelings of later married life. As our marriage matures, we become more aware of who we are. This generates apartness as well as togetherness.

when our questions and doubts are no longer fleeting
thoughts, but have instead become disturbing—

when one part of ourselves flashes a danger signal,
telling us that something is not right,

when the report of our total self is not yet in (we
can't think and feel as whole beings),

when we are strung-out and unable to affirm the other
person with all our emotion and affection,

when the devilish imp of yesterday bolts into our
minds to say, "This is not the way you felt when
you first married,"

when we begin to "pick," deliberately looking for the
negative rather than the positive,

our marriage is veering off the "life" path and into the "death" stretch.
It needs resurrection!

I'm not knocking feelings. Feelings are important. But we don't
pledge to love only when there is feeling; we pledge to love "for better
or worse, for richer or poorer, in sickness and in health." This vow
recognizes that feelings fluctuate; it also insists that we bring these
fluctuations into the safe harbor of a love decision. As we *decide*
to love, we will find an at-homeness with each other that frees us
to share our deepest desires and disappointments. We can even be
vulnerable. Highly charged encounters, negative expressions, even
threatened relationships will open a wide spectrum of new possibilities
for growth.

"I love you—I always have and always will, and I want to act
like it." That's decision. It's an important element in my picture
of marriage.

Married love looks like commitment. Jesus said, "For this reason
a man shall leave his father and mother, and be made one with his
wife; and the two shall become one . . ." (Matt. 19:5-6 NEB). That's
commitment.

Decision gets marriage headed toward life. Commitment provides
the necessary power for getting there.

But first, let's understand to whom the commitment is made. It isn't made to your marriage as an institution, but to your *mate in marriage!* Institutions aren't sacred; persons are!

For about eight years, I lived up to my commitment to the *institution* of marriage. You'd expect this of a clergyman—who else would be more loyal to institutions? I'm afraid I have to confess that my commitment to Jerry as my mate in marriage—to Jerry as a person—was not as great as my commitment to the institution. This is very strange. I mean, a minister is supposed to be sensitive to the needs of persons, isn't he?

My fear that we might drop a clue that ours wasn't a flawless marriage placed added strain on our relationship. First, we had to try to *make* our marriage flawless; then, that failing, we had to *picture* it as flawless. This was a terrific price to pay—but, then, no price would have been too great for preserving my professional stature. I could even conjure up God being on my side in that!

It was not so strange, then, that my first sharing at the deepest levels of spiritual intimacy would have been with anyone but Jerry. It happened that Everett Shostrom, a psychologist, and Gary Herbertson, a fellow minister, and I began writing a book, *The Manipulator and the Church.* In the book, we called for Christian actualization, which involves primarily honesty, awareness, freedom, and trust, and we called upon churches to provide the setting for this kind of growth through the establishment of Christian actualization groups. We tested our concept in my church. I was extremely reluctant to undertake this project because it would force me into a more honest encounter with Jerry. I was afraid of this even in the presumed sanctity of group sharing.

I suffered guilt because I recognized that I wasn't committed to Jerry as a person. She was different from me. I could without effort appreciate some of this difference. I valued her uniqueness, but in truth, I basically saw her as a reflection of myself. I was the minister; she was the minister's wife. I was the husband; she was the husband's wife. We related role to role, not person to person.

I made another discovery which threatened me. Jerry was much further along in many areas of growth than I. Almost "by nature" she possessed those traits I was trying to develop: honesty, awareness, freedom, trust, spontaneity. These were dimensions of her childlikeness that I had thwarted. I decided to commit myself to Jerry, person to person. It made all the difference in the world!

Love
  is decision
Marriage
  is commitment

I'm reminded of the man whose wife periodically suffered depressions. So he took her to the psychiatrist. "The treatment which I prescribe is simple," said the doctor. He went over, gathered the woman in his arms, and planted a lingering kiss on her lips. Then he stepped back and looked into the woman's glowing face.

"See," he said, "this is all that she needs."

"Okay, Doc," the husband said. "I'll bring her in on Tuesdays and Thursdays, but I gotta play golf on Saturdays."

Commitment to the institution, not to the person. We don't pledge our "troth" in wedding ceremonies nowadays, but we ought to. "Troth" has in it the strength of steel welded to steel. It means you've made a decision that has a lasting quality. What momentum is to movement, commitment is to decision. Commitment means today *and* tomorrow—even if it rains!

Married love looks like caring. The biggest heresy in marriage is alphabetical: Big I, little u. Marriage demands a Big We.

A cartoon of a young married couple in a marriage counselor's office captures the problem. The girl is clutching a teddy bear to her breast. "I think you know the problem, doctor," says the young man. "She keeps taking the teddy bear away from me." There's some selfishness at work in there somewhere.

Selfishness is a problem, but a more insidious problem is unconcern, *in which we don't care enough to care.*

"Will my marriage work?" is a lazy and selfish question. A more appropriate question is, "Will we work at our marriage?" Marriage is hard work, but if we really care about the other person, it's worth the effort.

To work at our marriage means to try to put life into it, to put caring on the dry bones of commitment.

Eric Fromm calls ours a "consumer society." Like a giant mouth, we devour experience and substance. There is real danger that we will consume our marriages.

Let's look at this consuming business. A big factor in our choice of a mate is our sense of deficiency. It was like this with me. My personhood was thwarted by my resentment toward my deprived background, my unwillingness to know and be known, and my lack of integrity (being together in one piece). So I needed a mate who would bolster my ego—someone I could protect, control, shape in my own image.

Jerry's need for security, her feelings of inferiority, her uncertainty of direction were met in the false image of strength, certainty, purpose, and direction which I projected. I didn't recognize it, but I was devouring Jerry's personhood at a terrible rate! Through the ministry of small groups, this came clear to me, and I decided to commit myself to caring for Jerry as a person!

If our relationship in marriage never goes beyond the level of need, we consume each other to make up for our own deficiency. Fromm says that "sex has become one of the main objects of consumption." We talk about "having" sex as we speak of "having" a glass of water. This limits sex to the animal level and we get animal returns.

Sex isn't supposed to be an act of consumption, but rather an experience of communion. This way, the *human* dimension is achieved: Two persons, committed to each other as persons care for each other's joy and fulfillment. Intercourse becomes the climax of a *love-making relationship*. It is the celebration of full-bodied, full-souled communion.

Most of the persons who come to me for counseling need more freedom to "dance" sexually than they now enjoy. I don't believe that God would have made us with a hunger for sex if he hadn't intended for us to fulfill ourselves. Yet, not so very long ago, the church seemed intent on blunting sex drives, resulting in many crippled personalities. Thank goodness we've come to the point where we suggest that anything is right in a married couple's sexual relationship so long as it is mutually meaningful and gratifying and does not hurt or harm either partner.

If in a *caring* marital situation, we can find the freedom to experience sex as something freely given, freely received, and freely enjoyed, then sex will not be reduced to consumption. It will be more than the physical coupling of two persons. In such a caring and carefree atmosphere, sex becomes the *joie de vivre*, or joy of life.

If we are to know and be known, we have to know ourselves as male or female; we have to accept and appreciate the maleness or femaleness of other persons.

There is a sense in which marriage is the submersion of two partial selves into each other, and from that submersion two whole selves are born.

Marriage is the submersion of two partial selves into each other and from that submersion two whole selves are born......

In *Love Story,* a remorseful and worried Oliver searches all over for Jenny and finally finds her at home, sitting at the top of the stairs.

"Jenny, I'm sorry—" he begins.

"Stop," she cuts him off. "Love means not ever having to say you're sorry."

Love Story is a beautiful drama of devoted love, but that aspect of it misses the nature of true love by a million miles. *Of course* love means saying you're sorry!

There is another necessary step, and that is to say, "Forgive me." To say "I'm sorry" is simply to acknowledge that you did something wrong—there's no transaction. But to say "Forgive me" is to move beyond an admission of being wrong and to declare, "I need your love in spite of this thing I've done to you. I place myself at your mercy." A transaction takes place, affording mutual satisfaction and growth.

Behind almost every difficulty in marriage is a communication problem. Reuel Howe says, "Dialogue is to love what blood is to the body. When the flow of blood stops, the body dies. When dialogue stops, love dies and resentment and hate are born. But dialogue can restore a dead relationship. Indeed, this is the miracle of dialogue: It can bring relationship into being, and it can bring into being once again a relationship that has died."

A marriage is only as viable as its communication is viable.

In our church, we have 60 to 70 marriages a year. As part of the preparation for marriage, we require two group counseling sessions and one or more private sessions. We stress sex and communication because we've found these can be major areas of fulfillment or failure.

I suggest a ritual for these newlyweds. Each month, on their anniversary date, each questions the other, "Well, how are we doing in our marriage?" I suggest that they engage in this exercise throughout their first year of marriage. Some continue it. There's probably little hesitancy to ask "how're we doing?" that first month, but if a couple waits a year to ask this question, all sorts of red flags pop up!

I wish someone had suggested this process to Jerry and me. So much time passed before we could communicate with each other on "how we were doing" that our attitudes solidified. The elapsing time produced a tendency to "sweat it out" or "pout it out" rather than to "talk it out."

Jerry and I have found that the best times for us to talk about things personal and important are when we're driving somewhere together and have an hour or so free of distractions, or when we are able to get away to a fresh setting (mountains or ocean) without the children. We seek out these opportunities to catch up on who we are and are becoming. To set aside such time is a decision to commit oneself to caring.

"But," some reader may protest, "what if I don't happen to feel like caring?"

My response is that our decision to enter into a loving relationship with another person should have the length of *commitment* attached to it. At times it may be necessary to act counter to our feelings of the moment. We may have to do things mechanically until they become spontaneous. Sometimes it's necessary to prime the pump, so to speak. Interestingly, once we have let down our barriers, we find sharing isn't so difficult, after all.

I don't know why we presume that we can be good partners in marriage without effort. We don't approach other relationships or activities this way. Yet, we take marriage for granted.

If we are *intentional* about our marriage, we will do whatever is necessary to bring the relationship to fruition. Jerry is a person who needs a lot of physical affection and frequent expressions of tenderness. I had been a person who was not expressive in this fashion. It pained Jerry to have to ask for this kind of attention. But when she did, a turning point came in our marriage. I began to act deliberately. Jerry knew that my actions were often mechanical. One night she said to me, "I don't ever want you to say, 'I love you, *too*.' "

You see, I had been *responding* to *her* words of love, rather than initiating such expressions. Usually, "I love you, *too*" doesn't have the zing to it that "I love you" has. We have to discipline ourselves to be spontaneous.

Some of us act as though our marriage were a cross to be carried in penance for, I suppose, falling in love. Nothing could be a greater travesty of the cross of Christ. Marriage *does* afford us an opportunity to experience the cross. We care enough to enter another person's life and share in it, even when to do so exacts pain and suffering. To care means I'm committed to be *with* and *for* my mate no matter what trial or tragedy befalls us. To care means that I cherish my mate and am willing to commit myself—my energies and my time—to her fulfillment.

□ BECAUSE

Because we care, we *notice.*

Because we care, we *listen.*

Because we care, we are *honest.*

Because we care, we *share.*

Because we care, we *act.*

□ BECAUSE

This is what married love looks like. It's the kind of love that can bring resurrection out of death. This kind of love takes the partner by the hand and leads him or her into a ballroom for a lifetime of dancing.

Chapter 7

See Here, I Am Worthy of Your Love

As our plane left California and started over the mountains and deserts of Arizona, I laid aside John Gardner's book *Self-Renewal* and reflected upon his assessment of young people: "Many have stopped learning in the religious or spiritual dimensions of their lives long before they graduate from college. . . . By their mid-thirties most will have stopped acquiring new skills or new attitudes in any central aspect of their lives."

Mr. Gardner's statement set a-spinning that old jukebox song, "Old Pappy Time Is A'Picking My Pocket." Old Pappy starts picking people's pockets while they're young. If Gardner is right, most young adults assume that their lives have been cast in bronze (iron, more likely) as rigid and fixed as when Baby's first shoes are made into metal bookends. With such an assumption, all that these young people can hope to do is to polish their lives a bit.

Usually, I don't spend much time looking out plane windows—I prefer to read or talk with someone. But we had left the smog of Southern California behind (sufficient reason to celebrate), and it was the kind of clear day on which you can see forever.

For some reason, I was spellbound by the physical features below me. My remoteness from them miniaturized them, but my mind's computer restored them to their natural size. There were chasms which had been gutted out by wildly rushing waters; jagged peaks were wearing little caps of snow, and highways circled mountains like pieces of thread binding a giant, brown package. In places, the terrain's contrasting colors suggested that Mother Nature had paused to wipe clean her brush upon an enormous earthen palette. But what struck me most were the vast stretches of barren ground, seemingly devoid of any life whatsoever. These deserts stretched almost interminably; only rarely could I find tiny clusters of buildings indicating people and community.

Then, in a mysterious experience of a type that is afforded us only occasionally, the Spirit moved in me, saying, "That's the way your life is, Maxie—a vast terrain of inner space, most of which is undeveloped."

My soul snapped to attention and listened to what was being said. When I came out of that Spirit-with-Self dialogue, I made a fresh decision to develop that vast terrain of inner space which was waiting to be cultivated.

My experience on the plane convinced me that power is available to us if we will only invite it. Actually, reflection and inner exploration ought to be an ongoing process rather than an occasional event. *Real living* is like that, you know. Birth doesn't end with the first surge of air into the baby's lungs; rather, he is born again each time a significant person or significant experience comes to him. At each intersection of life, he is born again. Birth is a process, not an event.

As a rule, physical growth comes naturally, although growth can sometimes be painful and be resented, especially by the lanky adolescent. But it's significant that in early adulthood, visible physical growth virtually stops except at the belt-line. And, at the same time, as John Gardner observes, *religious* and *spiritual* growth also tends to falter and then cease.

For the adult, growth won't just happen; we have to make it happen! Which isn't easy!

It costs a lot to be a person
    to be human
    to be loving
    to respond to that life-call
        that roars at the core
        of our being

It's all kind of helter-skelter
    life calls for death
    security demands risk
    at-homeness requires abandonment
    love means hurt

Knowing is tenuous
    for change is certain
    and doubt dogs a seeker's steps
    dawn and darkness hold hands like lovers

To plunge into life completely
    is our baptism
And to dance with fellow-plungers
    is our communion

Growth is the dynamic
    of true humanity
And joy of being
    is the reward.

...to plunge into life completely is our Baptism, and to share with fellow plungers is our Communion...

We have to decide to grow—to seek resurrection. But to make the decision to grow and to carry out the commitment is difficult because we aren't sure of our starting point. I am forever undergoing change; I am continuously *becoming.* I don't understand completely who I am right now, much less who I should become at some later time.

Viktor Frankl has been a prophet and hero to me during my "adolescence" of spiritual and emotional growth. The truth of one of his statements in *Man's Search For Meaning* stabs me, yet it comforts me:

> A human being is not one thing among others; *things* determine each other, but man is ultimately self-determining. What he becomes—within the limits of endowment and environment—he has made of himself. In the concentration camps, for example, in this living laboratory and on this testing ground, we watched and witnessed some of our comrades behave like swine while others behaved like saints. Man has both potentialities within himself; which one is actualized depends on decisions and not on conditions.

I wanted the courage to commit myself to growth, but at my emotionally immature stage, I also found myself desiring to do *nothing.* Often, I longed to take the path of least resistance, and, like a stick tossed into a rushing stream, permit myself to be carried wherever the currents of my environment directed. But that day on the plane, I came to a strange realization: I couldn't be even *this* free! I couldn't even let myself go. I was too uptight for that. I had never willingly permitted myself to be vulnerable—whenever there was the slightest rustle in the leaves about me, my ears came up, my pulse quickened, and I was prepared for either fight or flight. Permit myself to be carried along? No. I had to be in the driver's seat!

The only problem was, I didn't deserve to drive because I didn't know which way I was going. More importantly, I didn't know where I was going to end up. And, wherever I was going, I wasn't going to like it, anyhow.

As I sat viewing the earth from my airliner perch, I became aware that I was looking inward rather than outward. And I judged by what I found inside that I was too immature, too unreliable, to hold a driver's license and to travel life's roadways. I too often put the well-being of myself and others in jeopardy. In my anguish, I silently prayed, "Oh, God, I don't want to be a phony. Nobody wants to be a phony. I'm not so fearful of the truth about myself, which I am in this moment facing up to; my greater fear is that my self-protection machinery will blot out my self-view and block my intention to correct my faults. Dear God, don't let me go back to playing my little game!"

My game had been: "*See here, I am worthy of your love and acceptance!*"

You already know my history. My family was poor. Neither of my parents went to high school. If any of us five children had any shoots of cultural and creative growth within us, this potential had very little opportunity to develop.

In my rebellion against this background, I have spent a good part of my life *proving* myself to others. I have been a slavish worker, tirelessly bent on achieving and performing. I have driven myself mercilessly to success, a fear of failure constantly drawing from me more and more energy, and serving as a demanding taskmaster of my life.

Even in my sex life with my wife, I found myself thinking in terms of performance. I could not bear failure or the threat of failure, whatever my activity. Much of my energy was going into unproductive efforts, including the building of stages upon which I could perform. This was a neurotic effort on my part to prove myself to others—a desire to be accepted by them.

Who was I?

Was I the person I "really was" (whatever that meant) or the fictional fellow I was impersonating?

On that plane, I acknowledged that I had to find out who I was. I made a decision to commit myself to becoming the person that I could be, to discover the self I could trust, the self I could love and allow others to love, the self I could share. That confession and dedication might have died as had my other emotionally charged self-encounters except for two men. These two men invested themselves in my life and permitted me to invest in their lives.

A group of us ministers met weekly in the office of a psychologist, Everett Shostrom. We brought along sack lunches. We ate together and shared in conversation for two hours. Our stated purpose was to draw upon Ev's expertise and thereby become better counselors. It happened that Ev was working on the manuscript for a book called *Man the Manipulator*. From time to time, he read to us from the manuscript and asked us to help him to refine his method and presentation. You can't remain on the professional level when you are talking about manipulation—we all became personally involved. Painfully, I discovered that I was The Master Manipulator. I could serve as a model of many situations that Ev discussed. Beyond this, I found myself attempting to manipulate this group! I was trying to contribute more than anyone else—not to help Ev, but to prove my intellectual prowess.

This dawning of awareness mushroomed into blinding insight in an extension of this weekly relationship. As already indicated, Ev and I, with another minister, Gary Herbertson, collaborated in writing *The Manipulator and the Church*. In this project, we had to share of ourselves—we had to practice what we proposed to preach. In my encounters with these two men, I saw the ping-pong polarities of my being.

> I have pride
>   ... I am humble
> I am selfish
>   and unselfish
> I am assertive
>   yet dependent
> I love
>   ... I hate
> I admire
>   yet despise
> I am weak
>   ... I am dominating
> I trust myself
>   Yet am overly competitive

Fortunately, as I discovered my nature, I found that I could reveal both the "good" and "bad" dimensions of myself to others and still be accepted. This was a growth experience. And as I developed the courage and facility for sharing with these professional friends and with my wife, I became able to share (albeit less completely) with other persons.

I do not mean to gloss over the difficulty that I experienced as I attempted to lift myself to this kind of sharing. It was hard! And there was an extra degree of trauma in it for me because as I shared, I saw that I had been living a contradiction, a big lie! I had been *preaching* acceptance for a decade, but in fact I had not been able (1) to accept myself, (2) to accept others, or (3) to believe that I was acceptable in God's sight.

Now that I was able to unkink the knots in my life-support tube, I really came alive. For the first time, I recognized that my wife really loved me and accepted me. I saw that her commitment went beyond the exigencies of the day—it was written against a background of "forever." I saw that other people had come to know me and to love me. And God's love and forgiveness became real. I was able to *accept his acceptance!*

For the first time in my life, I could stand and face the world, eyeball to eyeball; I could face the ugly and the beautiful, the stranger and the friend, the domineering and the subservient. I could stand before God and everybody and say, "Here I am, *Maxie Dunnam!*" Not aggressively, yet without apology. Not proving myself, but simply *being.*

On reflection, I found that I had spent more of my time *proving* than *being.* "See here," we say, "I am worthy of your love and acceptance. And if you don't believe it (or even if you do), I'll prove it to you."

A dear friend of mine played this game in deadly earnest. As a child, she recognized that she wasn't as smart as one of her younger sisters or as pretty as the other. She had to prove herself in some way, and so she assumed the characteristic of being "strong." When other people went to pieces, she stood as solid as a rock. People could bring their problems and pour them into her ears. Her parents, sisters, other relatives, and friends encouraged this stance. The expression that she remembers most clearly from childhood and youth is, "Marj is the strong one!"

Marj carried this image of strength over into her marriage and parenthood. Now, at age 50, she is discovering the joy that can come with being accepted despite her weakness. In church groups, she has been able to fail and acknowledge failure. "Marj is the strong one" no longer haunts her and drives her to phoniness. Her marriage has found new life. Her husband, who fell into the snare of expecting perfection from her, has blossomed in his personhood because she is now evoking his gifts of strength and creativity, whereas before she had smothered him.

I call *"See here, I am worthy of your love and acceptance"* a game because to win is a hollow achievement. To love and accept on the basis of worthiness is not deserving of being called love and acceptance. The kind of love and acceptance that you can get by proving yourself will play out—and soon!

Yet we burn ourselves out trying to earn esteem and appreciation. That bag is too heavy to carry. Jesus says to us, "The Father loves you. You are accepted. And I love you, too, not on the basis of your merit, but simply because you are you." (That's a rather free translation.) We don't have to *prove,* we only have to *be.* We only have to respond, in faith, to Christ, the communicator of the Father's love.

Some games are fun. But this game is grim. I know. It made a mess of my life. The trouble is that it is directed outward rather than inward. This game left me no time for *self*-knowledge. The esteem and appreciation that we need is basically *self*-esteem and *self*-appreciation.

But a word of caution. You can't be forever proving yourself to *yourself* either. Just as we need to be free of over-dependency upon others, we also need freedom from self.

Let me share a personal experience:

In the midst of an exciting ministry at West Anaheim United Methodist Church, I received the most attractive job offer ever to come into my hands. I was invited to head a Christian training and retreat center. It was the kind of position I had always dreamed about. In this position, I would be associated with persons who were dear to me.

Have you ever anguished over deciding between two positions? For three weeks, I experienced torment.

I decided to continue in the local ministry. In the decision process, I was proud to discover how conscious I was of the pitfall of proving myself to others. But I discovered in the dark corners of my being a more insidious problem: *I wanted to prove myself to myself.* The country boy of my past stood before me, tugging nervously on his overalls' galluses and shifting uncomfortably from one foot to the other. He pleaded with me to accept the greater challenge and take the new job. "Prove to *me* that you can do it," he entreated.

He still had a grip on me, that poor country boy did. Culturally, economically, and educationally deprived, he had been pulling himself up, doggedly making his way along. I needed to show that barefoot exile from rural Mississippi that I could do it! It was an almost irresistable pull.

I don't claim that I am free, but I did win a round in that decision process. Isn't that about all that we can hope to do? With each successive round, we become more capable of dealing with the next bout.

To be locked into self is to be locked into "solitary," a lightless, airless, companionless dungeon. This is why Paul talked about "the whole body being built up." We can come to a mature realization of ourselves only in relationships. Resurrection is an experience which we obtain through sharing with others.

As I have indicated, insights into what makes me tick usually have come in times of crisis or during an intensity of feeling. Later, another challenge comes, permitting me to test what I have learned. Still another challenge permits me to reaffirm what I have come to realize and have subsequently tested.

In this and other chapters, I have indicated that recent experiences have permitted me to grow like Jack's beanstalk. Shortly after my showdown struggle with the proving game, the test for my new-found freedom came. I had the occasion to visit my mother and father, who are still living in rural Mississippi.

I didn't look forward to the trip. On previous visits, I felt uneasy and resentful; I came away suffering depression. Even though my father and mother had risen above the subsistence level of my boyhood, going home reminded me of everything that I had hated—all that I had been running away from.

I flew into New Orleans and borrowed a friend's car for the drive to Richton, Miss. The trip was two and one-half hours. Because of the self-communication process that I had begun, I used this time to chat with myself about home and what it meant to me. A peace descended upon me, and by the time that familiar landmarks came

To Love
and Accept
on the basis of
Worthiness
is not worthy of
being called
Love   and
Acceptance

into view, these symbols evoked positive and pleasant responses. I was able to cope with events and situations which heretofore had caused me anguish. Moreover, most of my thoughts were about happy times shared with family and friends. When I arrived, my parents paid scant attention to the E-type Jaguar I drove. (I hastened to identify it as the property of a friend.) We sat down to a meal that might today be characterized as "soul food." My parents showed less interest in the fact that I had just published a book than they did in my accounts of the most recent escapades of their five-year-old grandson. For once, I was sympathetic with their value system—I would have been disappointed if they had valued the Jaguar or the book above their grandson.

After supper, we sat and talked in relaxed fashion. I found myself inquiring about persons who had been important in my life. Many had died, and I felt a distinct sense of loss. Not all our talk was so somber. We chatted about some of the real "characters" of those parts and about the internal "fights" of the little Baptist church.

Next morning, before I departed, my father insisted that I accompany him on a walk around the pasture. Once it had been a field, plowed and tended by my brothers and me. How I had hated those sun-baked rows of corn and beans and those weedy terraces, but now I had a sense of belonging to that land. I had a sense of being on holy ground.

I discovered that I *could, should, would* go home again!

Going home had been a beautiful experience, largely because of a little boy who accompanied me. My companion was that grubby, "pore" little boy of my past. It was a joy to have him show me my homeplace and refresh in my memory the events which have contributed immensely to the man that I am today.

I drove back to New Orleans recognizing that I had experienced a great turning point in my life. Why, during my visit, I had hardly noticed my parents' transgressions against the English language. In former days, their errors would have driven me wild, but these parents—my parents—had given me something more precious than fancy language. They had given me love. If they could give me love in spite of their problems and inadequacies, I certainly ought to be able to share such love with my children!

I had even obtained information about my ancestors. I patted my coat pocket to be sure the piece of paper on which I had scribbled this information was there. Yes, I had a heritage. I had been born

close to the earth, of earthy parents. I had come from a long line
of simple, hard-working, God-fearing people. I realized that the primary meaning of time is that there are persons who become bridges
between the past and the future so that I may walk in the present
with meaning.

I recognized that I was able to celebrate this now-moment only
because I had become capable of trusting time itself. Formerly, I
had been in a no-man's land, between past and future, and there
was no peace to be found. But now time permitted me to go back
and forth and to relish present, past, and future.

What are the symbols which bring anxiety, fear, resentment to
your mind? Not a little runny-nosed, patched-pants boy, very likely.
But I'll venture that you have a relic of memory which pinches you
even today.

Become acquainted with these bothersome symbols. Accept them
as what they are—symbols. When you see that they cannot pain
you unless you let them hurt you, you have won half the battle.
The other half of the fight is: When you are assailed by these painful
memories, conjure up symbols which evoke a pleasant response.

You can't erase painful experiences, but you can learn to cope
with them expediently. When the little boy who begrudgingly and
achingly gathered corn and carried wood intrudes upon my mind,
I think of stone-bruises and parched throats, true. But then I look
beyond the hardships at the necessity for the little boy's parents
to have worked him like this, and at the contribution that this
acquaintance with hard work and hard workers has made to a minister
who now often suffers from a white-collar image. The burden becomes
a bit easier, too, when I conjure up a picture of this little boy and
his brothers slipping away and taking a dip in a nearby creek, wearing
nothing more than their innocence.

When I exercise this positive approach, what formerly seemed a
funeral becomes a celebration—a *resurrection.*

The change came when I recognized *"See here, I am worthy of
your love and acceptance"* for what it is—a game, and a poor one
at that.

Am I worthy? I don't have to prove that to you, do I? No. I'm
me. I'm learning to like me. I hope you like me, too. I have the
reassurance of many people who do. And God loves me! That alone
is enough to keep me dancing.

Chapter

Time and a Way of Trusting

One of the appeals of television's afternoon soap operas is that you don't get the conclusion today. Episodes may last for weeks or months, and before one of these stories-within-stories peaks out, the writer has already hooked you with the next episode, just beginning to unfold. There's always something to anticipate.

I'm glad that life itself is an unfinished story, a to-be-continued drama. To move from episode to episode is exciting—*if* you'll let yourself become excited.

I have been excited these last several years. I've discovered that as one episode merges into another, I can usually find within me the resources that I need. I have found a vast reservoir of potential.

Where I used to kick myself along, or drag myself, now I am able to walk like a man. I don't waste energy holding back, scolding, sulking. At times, I find myself *dancing!* I am fortunate, indeed!

As I have told you earlier, for the first seven or eight years of our marriage, I was committed to the *institution* of marriage rather than to Jerry as a person. This wasn't satisfactory to Jerry—not at first. But this style of relationship contains a certain amount of security, and once Jerry's hunger for a more personal relationship became less acute, she began settling into the old-shoe comfort of institutionalized security. (If I was committed to the *institution* of marriage, she wasn't likely to get hurt, was she?) Marriage or any other interpersonal relationship is an equation. It's dynamic. You alter one part of the system and the other parts have to come to a new way of relating. Jerry told me recently that when I started becoming plain Maxie Dunnam instead of "the Rev. Maxie Dunnam" or "Maxie Dunnam, 'pore' farm boy," her own living quarters began to rock. Then, with her playhouse of institutionalized marriage torn down, she found herself thrust out onto the frontiers of a real human relationship. We had to work out a new commitment to each other as persons.

What I want to say now is difficult to phrase, for I don't want to fall into the trap of "Big I, little u." I don't want to suggest that I forced Jerry to change or even led her to change, for these statements detract from her own role in finding herself and in finding a new relationship with me. During the time I was changing, Jerry was changing, too. Our equation maintained sufficient balance and sufficient momentum to hang together as its several elements shifted.

The affinity and interlockingness which permits persons to hang together under stress and to feel that the future together will be rewarding is *trust*.

You may suggest that trust is just another dimension of commitment, and in a sense this is so. But I think that trust has more of a two-way stretch within it. Trust means that I open the door to my life and let you walk in. Not only do I let myself be known, I even let myself be *intruded* upon.

I was in my study and my nine-year-old Kerry came in. I was very busy, and as I looked up, she no doubt read in my face irritation at being disturbed, as well as a parental "you've broken my rule" scowl because she hadn't knocked. I was about to reprimand her when, quick as a flash, she said, "I just wanted to tell you I love you."

As a mother's kiss makes a childhood hurt go away, so Kerry's words kissed away my annoyance. Had Kerry intended to come into my study and say these words, or did she say them on the spur of the moment to rescue herself from a scolding? It didn't matter! If I had questioned her, I would have knocked the petals off the blossom of love. I would have murdered Trust!

Most men prefer the hell
of a predictable situation
rather than risk the
Joy of an unpredictable one.

How difficult it is to trust somebody. Kerry had been giving us problems. She was an underachiever in school. Working with her nights had been mutually difficult. We all felt insecure. But we had, with great persistence and with the most love we could gather up, attempted to impress upon her that while we didn't like her poor work in school, we continued to like *her* very much. The past evening had been one of our closest sharing times—so close, I suppose, that now Kerry felt she could intrude upon her father's study and he would love her just the same. I'm glad I didn't muff it. In the glow of that moment in my study, Kerry and I "danced" in celebration of our great new relationship.

"You're Nobody Till Somebody Loves You." There's truth in that song title. My power to choose to love you or not to love you makes me a determining influence in your life; by the same process, you are a determiner in my life.

Trusting acknowledges that the equation may swing either way, but it says, "Come into my life," just the same.

You will recall the formula I worked out:

Living depends on loving,
loving depends on knowing,
knowing depends on risking.

The genius of that formula hangs on trust. You can't love, know, risk, unless you trust. Trust keeps the channels clear for interpersonal relation to spill through.

If I cannot trust Jerry—if I cannot trust her to respond to my feelings of the moment, I am in trouble. If I feel angry but cannot express this anger here and now, I will suppress it, but the anger doesn't go away—it sulks. Then I watch Jerry like a hawk, and when she does something that permits me to yell "Foul," I yell! If I had trusted Jerry in the first place, we might have worked through our difficulty with less strain and residual damage.

We need to trust persons. We also need to trust *time*.

My past had been like sour garlic and I had tried to spit it out. Also, I had drawn a line between past and present, and you can't do that. You have to embrace the unity of time. There is a reality which cuts across the artificial boundaries of past, present, and future. I was in such headlong flight from my past that *I was running clear through my present.* With an unacceptable past and an unavailable present, there was no place left for me but in the future. *One day,* I would get it all together—in the sweet by and by.

By now, I hope that you have come to grips with your own past, but let me point out that many people never do.

I knew a maiden lady who ventured out into the world but soon retreated to the house in which she had been born. This became her life-house. Nostalgia became her language. The South had never been defeated—chivalry lived on! She was a Southern lady, and, "See here, I am deserving of your respect (if not your love and acceptance)."

I know a man who, in a fit of anger, banished his son. He is stuck in another kind of life-house. His house is haunted by an act which he has judged irreparable. But, given a dimension of trust, the relationship might be repaired.

Many of us are stuck in houses-of-the-past. I broke out of mine, geographically, but in a more realistic sense, I still carried it about on my shoulders. I remained enclosed by the walls of what had been.

The past may limit us—for example, I may never overcome my educational deficit (in the sense of what might have been). But my past should not and must not limit my *personhood.* In spite of my past, I can be as much a *person* as the next guy.

On occasion, as I review this emerging manuscript, I have a nagging fear that I am making my self-growth seem too pat. You know, I went off into the mountains, and presto! I was changed. I was walking down a street looking at windows and a great truth came to me. I met a man on a plane and my life hasn't been the same since then.

I don't want to detract from the sublime moments of truth which suddenly break in on us—we *are* sometimes blinded with insight (as Paul was) and we *are* gripped by a command to "Follow me!" But for balance I must reiterate that my own growth-experience has been a *process*—not just some *steps,* and never an *arrival. It has been, and is, a journey and a pilgrimage.*

At the risk of oversimplifying, let me outline the way I have seen my pilgrimage going:

First, I have had to acknowledge, examine, and accept my pains from the past.

Second, I have had to acknowledge, accept, and appreciate the gifts that I have received through the grace of God and the grace of other persons.

Third, I have had to make crucial decisions.

Fourth, I have had to become able to trust the persons who are important to me, whom I call "my significant others."

If you have already moved through the stage of becoming able to cope with your pains of the past (we never get to the point where we don't have to rework our past), then move on and look at your gifts.

I had been so intent upon my deprivation, I was blind to gifts received from my parents. Now when I think of what my parents mean to me, I sing for joy. They gave me a feeling for people, a commitment to truth, a potential for trusting. They had trusted me, but I hadn't recognized it. They were poor in terms of cultural and educational possessions, and so they did for me the only thing that they could do well: They loved me! How beautiful!

Take your past. Turn it over—look at the "flip" side—the "gifts" side. A recording is worth having if only *one* side "sends" you, isn't it?

Decisions come in two flavors. There are the decisions that have already been made, and these have to be reviewed, or some of them do. And then there are the decisions which are yet to be made.

To make decisions solely on the basis of "what has been" is a perversion. The better perspective is "what is coming to be." A good mix of past, present, and future.

The dwellers-in-the-future are as pitiable as the once-upon-a-timers. They are obsessed with tomorrow's promises and invest their total resources in a dream world of the future. They are unmindful that they will drag into this never-never land of the future all of the impediments and infirmities of their unresolved present and past. My child's-eye-view of religion was a pie-in-the-sky picture. I remember the songs we sang: "In the sweet by and by" and "When we all get to heaven, what a day of rejoicing that will be." These songs dismissed the goodness of *now* and focused instead on streets paved with gold and mansions filled with goodies. But let's not grow too smug. Many of us have failed to carry our mature approach over into the everyday aspects of our lives.

At the same time, there is an opposite sort of perversion. Like the horse with blinkers to keep him from looking to either side or to the rear, the "now" generation grips *today* blindly. I see this fault in extreme existentialist positions, which insist that the immediacy of now is the only reality. Youth has reason to be impatient with the older generation's worship of the past and future, but often they overcompensate, saying that the only reality is now. Some famous thinkers are victims of this malady. One of them is Abraham Maslow. He has influenced me deeply in other matters, but I think he misses the mark in his book *Motivation And Personality* when he defines authentic existence after the model of the child:

> . . . The consequence is that the child is totally without past and future. If one expects nothing, if one has no anticipations or apprehensions, if in a certain sense there is no future, because the child is moving totally 'here-now', there can be no surprise, no disappointment.
>
> One thing is as likely as another to happen. This is 'perfect waiting' and spectatorship without any demands. This is all related to my conception of the creative personality as one who is totally here-now, one who lives without future or past.

That isn't for me. Who wants that? *Spectatorship without demands. No surprises?* Whether we like it or not, whether we choose to deal with it or not, *we have a past.* Moreover, after a few hour's sleep tonight, I will awaken to a tomorrow which will then be my today. So I have a future.

I don't have to live in the past in order for the past to have meaning. What I have to do is to appropriate the meaning of the past for my here and now. I will see that my past affords me certain opportunities; but if I am realistic, I will also recognize that I have certain limitations growing out of my past.

I am here and now. I draw upon my past. But some of my here and now is spent anticipating, expecting, planning, hoping, dreaming. Only as I contemplate the future with trust can I be truly spontaneous.

Gestalt therapy captures this "big picture." The "camera" of our being focuses sharply on the present, which deserves our closest attention. But the past and future also appear in the photograph. They are less distinct, even blurred, but they are there!

Rabbi Abraham Heschel in *Who Is Man* speaks to this: "The authentic individual is neither an end nor a beginning but a link between ages, both memory and expectation. Every moment is a new beginning within a continuum of history. It is fallacious to segregate a moment and not to sense its involvement in both past and future. Humbly the past defers to the future but it refuses to be discarded. Only he who is an heir is qualified to be a pioneer."

For me, it boils down to this: I must trust *time;* to narrow it down, I must trust *my lifetime.* I have roots in the past, but I am not root-bound. I salute the future, but I do not pledge my total allegiance to it. And this puts me mostly in the *present,* where I really belong— where I can really *be!*

Paul knew this. In the throes of suffering, he declared, "I leave the past behind, and with hands outstretched for whatever lies ahead, I go for the goal." Paul had roots—he was a "Jew of the Jews" in the best tradition. And he was mindful of a better tomorrow. But Paul lived in the present moment: "For me to live *is* Christ."

That's where I am. The past is accepted and either affirmed or forgiven. The future is open and I reach toward it with hope. I'm getting it all together—the present, past, and future; knowing and being known; the decision-making; the commitment; the investment. Christ is at the center, leading me to a new level of integrity, integrating the past and future into a grace-full *now.* And the enabling element is trust. I couldn't be carefree enough to dance if I couldn't— and didn't—trust.

In seeking to trust, I've seen this sort of cycle working in my life:

I feel rejection
    which brings
Feelings of worthlessness
    which brings
Self-hate
    which makes me
Seek escape by
    hiding from others
    refusing to share
    becoming defensive
        which causes
Others to react against my defenses
        which brings on
Further feelings of
Rejection
        which starts the cycle again.

There is another cycle in my life that works like this:

I trust myself as
    worthwhile
        having something to offer
            which causes me to
Affirm myself
    which enables me to
Open myself and
    share with others
        who respond with
Love and acceptance
    which verifies
My self-worth
    which inspires me to
Trust myself
And the cycle starts all over again.

I've found that my self-hate, for the most part, comes out of feeling that I have been rejected by others. At the same time, I have learned how to love myself through my relationships with others. Again, the formula presents itself:

> Living depends on loving,
> loving depends on knowing,
> knowing depends on risking.

Once we break the initial barrier of fear—fear that we won't be accepted because we aren't worthy of acceptance—we become able to risk. We are able to risk because we trust others to respond to our needs and to our offers of friendship, and to respond out of a relationship that has been there all the while—our common humanity. *Change* isn't so threatening when it is approached as *growth; death* isn't so frightening when it is approached as *rebirth*.

At the opening of this book, I told about the twangy song that grabbed me that cold night in the roadside cafe: "Old Pappy Time Is A'Picking My Pocket." More recently, I hear another catchy song:

> Everybody wants to go to heaven,
> But nobody wants to die.

I've told you where I am. I stand here in the present and say without boast or apology, "Here I am, *Maxie Dunnam.*" I am aware of the tracks behind me; indeed, I have retraced them and they do not hound me any more. I face the future, and I rest assured that it will be good—even heavenly. But I'm not so captivated by the future that I wish to rush there *right now!*

I don't want to slink back into my past; I don't want to rush into my future. For the moment, let me stand here and relish my present. But even as I stand here, I am dying. *But I am also being reborn!* I'm engaged in a process. It has all the excitement of a game, but it has a reality and meaning that a game can never have.

Thank you for coming along on my dancing trip. We started out going to a funeral, but we journeyed to a resurrection!

Birth is a
Process
and to be
Fully Born
is the
Aim of Life

The real test of a man
as he faces life
is whether he
runs, fights, whimpers or

dances

The Magic Kingdom

There are some things that I do with my children out of a sense of duty and with great effort. Disneyland isn't one of them.

We live only 10 minutes from Disneyland, and we go there twice a year, on average. Despite this familiarity, I always enter Disneyland with keen anticipation and I never leave disappointed.

On my family's last visit, I was standing there in the Magic Kingdom gawking at this monument to man's imagination and technological abilities. Two ladies walked right into me! "Pardon me," I said. (You see, I haven't lost all of my Southern heritage.) They didn't even see me! I don't think they saw *anything!* They were knitting.

I don't knit, but I appreciate this craft (even as therapy) and I enjoy wearing knitted sweaters. I do confess that I have this "thing" about people who knit when I'm up speaking—I have doubts about anyone concentrating on two things at one time.

But these ladies could knit while walking! (Until people like me should get in their way.) Maybe they could even knit while riding the bobsleds of the "Matterhorn."

While these ladies impressed me with their knitting ability, I'm afraid that they totally missed the magic of the Magic Kingdom. And while I hope that they finished those sweaters or shawls or whatever, I also hope that someday they'll return to Disneyland *without their needles and yarn* and permit themselves to be thrilled by the Magic Kingdom.

I've poked a bit of fun at little old ladies and at knitting. Even in these days of Women's Lib and a renaissance of arts and crafts, nobody is likely to scold me—*except myself!*

Lord, I don't know why those ladies
      were knitting so intently.
      There was so much to be
      wide-eyed at.
I wonder if they missed any stitches?
Knit one, purl two.
The shawl emerged
      but they missed the "Magic Kingdom"
Wow!
That's what I've done.
I've missed the Magic Kingdom—
      the kingdom of now.

I missed it by being
      so preoccupied with the past.
The "hound of hell"
      demanded all my attention.
      Why haven't I realized
      that his bark was worse than his bite?
The bark was the frightening thing.
      So I ran
      I fought
      I whimpered

Then remorse set in
   resentment
   regret
   bitterness
   guilt.
All my energy was required
   running from
   or fighting
   that "hound of hell."
Knit one, purl two,
   and I passed through the now
   missing the Magic Kingdom.

The future robbed me, too.
I closed my ears to the hound's bark
   and listened to tomorrow's siren song.
Stars were in my eyes
   getting out of Richton
   graduating from college
   finishing theology school
   moving to the next church
   earning more money
   gaining professional status
   publishing that first book.

The sparkling stars of tomorrow
blinded me to
balmy sun
mystic moon
dashing waves
love-lighted eyes
inquisitive frown
knowing smile
awareness
Knit one, purl two,
and I passed through the now
missing the Magic Kingdom.

Forgive me, Lord,
I heard
but I didn't listen-
I looked
but I didn't see.
"The Kingdom is *at hand.*"
"The Kingdom is *within you.*"
"*Today* is the day of salvation."
"*Now* is the acceptable time."
NOW. . . .
the Magic Kingdom
knit one, purl two?
Forgive me, Lord.

living

knowing

risking

ACKNOWLEDGMENTS

Book Page

6   From "Childhood" by Henri Percikow. Reprinted by permission of the author.

15   From "To A Dancing God" by Sam Keene. Published by Harper and Row Publishers, Inc., 1970.

17, 18   From "Good Lord, Where Are You?" by Leslie F. Brandt, copyright 1967 by Concordia Publishing House. Used by permission.

19   From "The Intimate Marriage" by Howard and Charlotte Clinebelle. Published by Harper and Row, 1970.

22   From "Why Am I Afraid to Tell You Who I Am?" by John Powell, S. J. Published by Argus Communications, 1969.

43   From "Little Gidding" by T. S. Eliot, published in "Four Quartets." Copyright 1943 by Harcourt Brace and Company. Reprinted by permission.

45   From "The Self In Pilgrimage" by Earl A. Loomis. Published by Harper and Brothers, 1960.

46, 47, 48   From "The Velveteen Rabbit" by Margery Williams. Reprinted by permission of Doubleday and Company, Inc.

64   From "The Manipulator And The Church" by Maxie Dunnam in collaboration with Gary J. Herbertson and Everett L. Shostrom. Published by Abingdon Press.

85   From "The Miracle of Dialogue" by Reuel Howe. Published by the Seabury Press, 1963.

88   From "Self-Renewal" by John Gardner. Published by Harper & Row, 1965.

91   From "Man's Search For Meaning" by Viktor E. Frankl. Published by Washington Square Press, 1963.

111   From "Motivation And Personality" by Abraham Maslow. Published by Harper and Row Publishers, Inc., 1954.

112   From "Who Is Man?" by Abraham Heschel. Published by Stanford University Press, 1965.